Book B

A Complete Course for Key Stage

CONNECTIONS

Libby Ahluwalia, Ann Lovelace, Jon Mayled, Joe Walker, Joy White

Acknowledgements

The publishers would like to thank the following individuals, institutions and companies for permission to reproduce copyright images in this book:

Cover photos reproduced courtesy of Photodisc (top left, top right & bottom right) and Corbis/Barnabas Bosshart (bottom left).
Libby Ahluwalia p66, 67, 69, 71, 72, 75; Amnesty International p41; Associated Press/ Stringer Norbert Schiller p35 (right); Christian Aid p41; Circa Photo Library p45 (top), 8, 70; Circa Photo Library/John Smith p48, 49, 73, 74; Corbis/Tony Arruza p24 (bottom right); Corbis/Dave Bartruff p55; Corbis/Morton Beebe p60; Corbis/Annie Griffiths Belt p18 (top right); Corbis/ Nathan Benn p37 (bottom); Corbis/Dean Bennett/ Eye Ubiquitous p77; Corbis/Bettmann p4 (bottom); Corbis/Bettmann p5 (top right); Corbis/Christie's Images for *The Adoration of the Magi* by Andrea Mantegna p9; Corbis/ChromoSohm Inc. p15; Corbis/Michael Cole p4 (lower middle); Corbis/Howard Davies p40 (top); Corbis/Laura Dwight p11 (bottom); Corbis/Ric Ergenbright p19 (bottom right); Corbis/ Macduff Everton p37 (top); Corbis/Mitchell Gerber p23 (top left); Corbis/Lynn Goldsmith p43 (bottom); Corbis/Philip Gould p24 (bottom left); Corbis/Lindsay Hebberd p45 (bottom); Corbis/Richard Hutchings p25; Corbis/Kelly-Mooney Photography p24 (top); Corbis/David Lees p24 (middle); Corbis/Farrell Grehan p14; Corbis/Kevin R Morris p18 (bottom left); Corbis/Richard T Nowitz p18 (bottom right), 56; Corbis/Charles O'Rear p18 (top left); Corbis/Christine Osborne p19 (top right); Corbis/Tim Page p54; Corbis/Philadelphia Museum of Art p47; Corbis/The Purcell Team p24 (top right); Corbis/Lee Snider p10, 52; Corbis/Ted Spiegel p58; Corbis/Vince Streano p5 (top left); Corbis/Peter Turnley p5 (bottom), 38 (top); Corbis/David H Wells p63; Corbis/Jennie Woodcock; Down's Syndrome Scotland p41; EMPICS Sports Photo Agency p4 (top); Sally and Richard Greenhill p43 (top); Hulton Archive p35 (left); ICOREC/Circa Photo Library/© Barrie Searle p3; Islamic Relief p41; National Gallery for *Adoration of the Shepherds*, by Luca Signorelli p7; Oxfam p41; PA News Photo Library p4 (upper middle), 23 (bottom right), 38 (bottom), 40 (bottom); Reflections Photolibrary p11 (top); Rex Features/PNS p34; Diane Whitfield p31; World Jewish Relief p41.

Every effort has been made to trace and acknowledge ownership of copyright. The publishers will be glad to make suitable arrangements with any copyright holders whom it has not been able to contact.

Orders: please contact Bookpoint Ltd, 130 Milton Park, Abingdon, Oxon OX14 4SB. Telephone: (44) 01235 827720. Fax: (44) 01235 400454. Lines are open from 9.00 - 6.00, Monday to Saturday, with a 24 hour message answering service. You can also order through our website www.hodderheadline.co.uk

British Library Cataloguing in Publication Data
A catalogue record for this title is available from the British Library

ISBN 0 340 80486 6

First Published 2002
Impression number   10 9 8 7 6 5 4 3 2
Year   2008   2007   2006   2005   2004   2003

Copyright © 2002 Libby Alhuwalia, Ann Lovelace, Jon Mayled, Joe Walker, Joy White

Typeset by Sarah Williams.
Printed in Italy for Hodder & Stoughton Educational, a division of Hodder Headline Ltd, 338 Euston Road, London NW1 3BH.

CONTENTS

text message.........

The history of the Jewish people has been full of ups and downs. Jews often look back at the reign of King David as being one of the best times in the past. Jews lived peacefully together in the Promised Land, and were ruled by a king who was successful in battle and was (usually) wise. David's son Solomon built a wonderful Temple in Jerusalem where God could be worshipped properly in the ways set out by the Bible.

However, the good times did not last. Weaker kings ruled after David, and the Jews did not always win their battles. Sometimes they were sent away into exile in other countries, and ever since, there have been Jews living in all different parts of the world, rather than together in the land promised to them. The Temple was totally destroyed and the Jews could no longer worship there.

*'For to us a child is born
to us a son is given,
and the government will be on his shoulders.
And he will be called
Wonderful Counsellor, Mighty God,
Everlasting Father, Prince of Peace.
Of the increase of his government and peace
there will be no end
He will reign on David's throne
And over his kingdom,
establishing and upholding it
with justice and righteousness
from that time on and for ever.'*

(Isaiah 9:6–7)

Jews believe that the Messiah has not yet come. They believe that before the Messiah will come, they have to make the effort to obey the laws of the Torah. When God chooses the right time, first Elijah will come back to tell the people that the Messiah is here, and then the Messiah himself will arrive. He will gather together all the faithful Jews, and then they will go through the Golden Gate into Jerusalem. There will be a new time when Jews live together in Israel again, just as they were promised; and the Temple will be rebuilt. To show that they are ready for the Messiah, Jews often leave a place for Elijah at festivals and celebrations – they set a place for him at the table, leave the door open for him, pour him a glass of wine and save him a chair.

One of the important beliefs of Judaism is that one day, a 'Messiah' will come and put everything right. Instead of turning away from God and being distracted by greed, selfishness, cruelty and other kinds of wrong, people will be led by the Messiah to a new understanding of God. The Messiah will rule over the Jews as a whole nation again, and the people will be obedient to God's commandments and live peacefully. The Jewish scriptures, known to Christians as the Old Testament, describe the Messiah as a person chosen by God to bring about these changes:

Language for learning

Messiah – the anointed one; the person chosen by God to lead the people into a new time of peace

Prophet – someone chosen to pass on messages from God to the people

Christians however, believe something different. They believe that there is no need to carry on waiting for the Messiah – they think that he has already come. Christians believe that Jesus was the Messiah, the person chosen by God to begin a new time of peace.

The Big Picture

In this section we will be looking at what Christians believe about Jesus, what he was like, and why Christmas is an important Christian festival.

At Passover each year, Jews keep a glass of wine ready for Elijah,
in case he returns to the world during their celebrations.

Lots of people have heroes that they believe were really special people. They might admire a great footballer of the past such as George Best, or a political leader such as Nelson Mandela, or someone who started something important such as Florence Nightingale who began the nursing profession in the UK. Religions also have important leaders who are greatly admired by all the believers: for example, Jews admire Abraham and Moses, Buddhists admire Gautama the Buddha, Sikhs admire the ten Gurus, and Muslims admire Muhammad (pbuh). But all of these people are believed to have been nothing more than human beings like the rest of us, even though they had very special qualities and did very special things.

Christians believe something different about Jesus. Although Christians admire Jesus as an example to follow, they think that Jesus was a lot more than just an ordinary man.

Christians believe that Jesus was **God incarnate**, which means that they believe that when Jesus was born, God actually came to earth to be born as a human. (The word 'incarnate' means 'made flesh'; it comes from the Latin 'carne', meaning 'flesh' – think of carnivores, which are flesh-eating animals, or chilli con carne, which is chilli with meat.)

✋ STOP &💡Think ❓

➤ If you had to choose five people that you think everyone should admire, who would you choose and why?

4

The Bible tries to explain this idea in different ways.

Paul, in his letter to new Christians at Philippi, writes about Jesus *'who, being in the very nature of God, did not consider equality with God something to be grasped, but made himself nothing, taking the very nature of a servant, being made in human likeness. And being found in appearance as a man, he humbled himself and became obedient to death – even death on a cross'* (Philippians 2:6–8). Paul was saying that Jesus shared the same nature as God, but even though he could have had great powers, he chose instead to be made into a human being and to suffer in the world like everyone else. Paul wanted to show that this was something Jesus had meant to do; it wasn't forced on him.

John, the gospel writer, describes Jesus as the Word of God, made into a human being: *'The Word became flesh and made his dwelling among us. We have seen his glory, the glory of the One and Only, who came from the Father, full of grace and truth'* (John 1:14). John's writing is often full of mystery and poetry; here he seems to be saying that by looking at Jesus, it is possible to understand something about God, because Jesus was the Word of God come to earth.

text message.........

Christians have discussed, for many centuries, how Jesus could have been both God and human at the same time, and there are many different ideas about how this could have been possible; but most Christians believe that it is a mystery, too deep for humans ever to understand completely.

➤ What do Christians believe that God is like? Do you think it is possible for a human being to have some, or any, of these qualities?

The gospel writers Matthew and Luke both tell stories about the birth of Jesus. The stories are not quite the same, probably because they heard about Jesus from different sources; but both Matthew and Luke try to show that even when he was born, there was something unusual about Jesus, which set him apart from other people. Matthew and Luke both try to show that Jesus was the Messiah, sent from God as the person that the Jews had been expecting for so long.

Luke begins the story by telling how the angel Gabriel was sent to Mary in Nazareth, to announce to her that she was going to be the mother of God's Son. Mary was afraid and did not understand how it could happen, because she was still a virgin. She was promised to a man called Joseph, but they were not yet married. The angel told her that the baby would be born by the power of the Holy Spirit, and promised:

Luke tells how Mary went with Joseph to Bethlehem when the baby was about to be born. The Roman government had decided to make a register of all the citizens so that they could be taxed, and everyone had to travel to the place their relatives came from, for the register. Bethlehem, Joseph's town, was a 'city of David', which was important to the gospel writers because they wanted to show that Jesus was fitting the picture of the Messiah that they had been given by the prophets.

When Joseph and Mary arrived in Bethlehem, all the rooms in the inns were already taken. Mary was about to give birth, so an inn–keeper took pity on the couple and allowed them to stay in his stable. In the night, Jesus was born.

According to Luke's gospel, the first people to come and visit the baby Jesus were shepherds, who heard the news of the birth from angels, and left the hillside to come and see the Messiah.

'He will be great and will be called the Son of the Most High. The Lord God will give him the throne of his father David, and he will reign over the house of Jacob for ever; his kingdom will never end.'

(Luke 1:33)

- Look at the story in Luke 1:26–38, where the angel Gabriel visits Mary. What does the angel say to Mary, to tell her that Jesus will be someone special? The angel tells Mary three things that her baby will be called – what are they?

text message.........

The prophet Micah promised the people that the Messiah would come from Bethlehem. He said:

But you, Bethlehem Ephrathah,
though you are small among the clans of Judah,
out of you will come for me
one who will be ruler over Israel.

(Micah 5:2)

PAUSE & RECORD

- Look at Luke 2:8–20. What did the angels tell the shepherds about the baby? How did the shepherds react at first? What did they do after they had seen Jesus?

'The Adoration of the Shepherds', by Luca Signorelli shows Joseph on the right, and the shepherds on the left. In the background, you can see the people going to be registered and taxed. Notice how the artist makes the baby Jesus the focus of the painting: even the animals are looking at him.

Matthew's gospel tells the story of Magi, traditionally translated as 'Wise Men', who saw a star in the east and knew that something special had happened – presumably they were experts in astrology. They followed the star to find the baby they believed was going to be 'King of the Jews', and the star stopped right over the house where Jesus was living. They gave him three gifts: gold, frankincense and myrrh. All of these things were expensive, and came from far away places. Frankincense is a perfumed oil, and myrrh was used for embalming dead bodies, which seems a strange gift to bring for a new baby. Many people think that these gifts had special, symbolic meanings. One suggestion is:

Gold – this was to represent the belief that Jesus is a king.

Frankincense – this was to represent the sacrifice that Jesus would make, because it smells sweet and the Bible says that God likes a sweet–smelling sacrifice.

Myrrh – this was to represent bitterness (myrrh tastes extremely bitter) and death.

No one knows how many Magi there were, because Matthew doesn't tell us, but traditionally people have imagined that there were three, because there were three gifts.

STOP & Think

➤ Many people, in the past and in the present, look at stars to try and find out the future. Some people look at horoscopes every day. Do you know your star sign? Do you think that it is possible for people to tell the future by looking at the stars?

Christians celebrate the visit of the Magi on 6 January, and the festival is called Epiphany, which means 'showing forth'.

Matthew and Luke tell quite different stories about the birth of Jesus, but both of the gospel writers tried in their own ways to show that Jesus was the Messiah the Jews had been waiting for.

PAUSE & RECORD

- Look in 1 Kings 10:10. What did the Queen of Sheba bring when she came to visit Solomon? If you were going to give something to a king or queen, what do you think would make a good present, and why?

Rewind

The Magi believed that they were looking for the 'King of the Jews'. Jesus never called himself King of the Jews, but in Matthew's gospel, other people gave him this title. Look at Matthew 27:37 to see when this was.

In this picture, 'The Adoration of the Magi', by Andrea Mantegna, the artist has shown the Magi as representing the three 'ages of man'. One is young, one is middle–aged and one is old. He has also shown them as coming from three different ethnic groups. One is black, one is Asian and one is white. What do you think the artist was trying to say when he chose to paint the Magi like this?

STOP & Think

➤ In the stories of Jesus' birth there are several supernatural, miraculous events, that show that Jesus was no ordinary baby – for example, an angel appeared to his mother to announce his birth. What other features of the story are miraculous? Do you think that these features say something important about Jesus – or do you think that they just make the stories difficult to believe?

Strictly speaking, Easter is the most important Christian festival, because it celebrates the resurrection of Jesus. But in many countries, Christmas is the main festival of the year, when people make preparations for weeks in advance, decorate their homes, give each other presents and eat special food. Many people do all these things at Christmas even if they have no religious beliefs at all, just for the fun of it.

Christmas is celebrated on 25 December, to remember the birth of Jesus, although Jesus was probably not born on that day. Christians adapted a midwinter festival which had existed since pagan times. It was celebrated in the middle of winter as a way of trying to persuade the sun to come back and the days to get longer again. Lots of evergreen leaves were used to show that life had not gone away completely in the dark winter months. Christians used this date for their own festival to celebrate the birth of Jesus.

The time before Christmas is known as **Advent**. For four Sundays before Christmas, Christians light candles to show their belief that Jesus is the Light of the World. During Advent, many people get ready for Christmas by buying presents for each other, cooking special food, and having parties – even if they are not Christians themselves.

On Christmas Day, they open their presents, have a special Christmas dinner, and perhaps get together with family and friends.

STOP & Think ?

> ➤ Why do you think that many people celebrate Christmas even if they have no religious beliefs of their own?

Christians often go to special services in church at Christmas. The children sometimes put on Nativity Plays, where they act out the story of the birth of Jesus in Bethlehem and the visits of the shepherds and the Magi. They sing Christmas carols, and this is often a time of year when they do something for charity, such as giving money to a shelter for the homeless.

Using evergreen to decorate homes at Christmas dates back to pagan times.

At Christmas, children often act out the story of the birth of Jesus.

Christmas is an important time of year for many people. It's an opportunity to see family members, and a time to keep in touch with people by sending cards and presents. But for Christians, Christmas is special because it marks the time when God came into the world, choosing to be born to an ordinary couple and to live in the world with everyone else, experiencing all the joys and suffering that human life has to offer. The birth of Jesus shows Christians that God is not too far away, but is willing to come and be a part of life in this world.

Christians believe that when Jesus was born, God came to live in the world as an ordinary human being.

11

text message.........

The Bible doesn't say much about what happened to Jesus when he was a child and a teenager. There is one story about Jesus at the age of twelve, told in Luke's Gospel, but nothing else. The Bible doesn't say what Jesus looked like, but there are many stories about things that Jesus said and did.

PAUSE & RECORD

- Look at Luke 2:41–52. What happened in the story? What do you think Luke was trying to tell his readers about Jesus, when he chose to include this story?

Jesus was well known as a teacher. Sometimes his followers called him 'rabbi', which means 'teacher'.

The Gospels tell how Jesus (when he was an adult) was tempted by the Devil to become wealthy and powerful, but he refused. Jesus was baptised by John the Baptist, and then he began teaching and performing miracles. He was well known as a healer, and people used to come to Jesus hoping to be cured of illnesses.

Jesus' teaching

Jesus taught about many different things – he told people how to pray, how to behave towards people in authority, how to treat the poor, and how everything would be different in the Kingdom of God. Jesus taught people that they should love one another. They should not just care about their families and their friends, but should treat everyone as a neighbour, even people who were strangers and enemies. Jesus often taught in parables, which are stories which illustrate a message.

Jesus the miracle worker

Christians believe that Jesus performed miracles. The Gospels tell stories of how Jesus turned water into wine at a wedding, and how he fed five thousand people with just five loaves and two fishes. In the Bible, Jesus made blind people see again, and people who had been paralysed got up and walked – he even raised Jairus' daughter and a man called Lazarus back to life after they had died. The Gospel writers wanted to demonstrate that Jesus really was the Messiah – he had special powers from God, and showed in his miracles what the world would be like when the Kingdom of God came.

Jesus the suffering servant

The Jews expected a Messiah who was going to be a hero and conquer their enemies. Jesus, instead, taught people to love their enemies, but he was still unpopular with many people. Some didn't like his teaching, because they thought that he was criticising them. Other people thought that he was dangerous, in case his followers got together and started riots. Jesus' enemies arrested him, and he was sentenced to death by crucifixion. If Jesus really did have special powers to perform miracles, perhaps he could have escaped death somehow, but instead he was nailed to a cross, where he died. Christians believe that Jesus did this out of obedience to God, and because he knew that it was the only way to build a new relationship between God and the rest of the world.

Jesus the Risen Lord

According to the Gospels, the story didn't end when Jesus died. Three days after his death, some women went to the place where Jesus was buried, to look after his body in the traditional way. But when they arrived at the tomb, the heavy stone, which had been rolled across the entrance to seal it up, had been moved away. The tomb was empty. The women were told that Jesus had risen from the dead. After the women had told Jesus' other friends what they had seen and heard, Jesus appeared to them, and they knew it was really true that he had risen from the dead. He showed them the nail marks in his hands, and told them that they were to go out and share their faith with the rest of the world. Then he left them and went back into heaven.

Christians believe that Jesus sacrificed himself for the rest of the world.

1

WHAT DOES JESUS MEAN FOR CHRISTIANS TODAY?

What do Christians mean when they talk about being 'saved'?

Christians believe that God came into the world when Jesus was born. They believe that God chose to live as a human, even though he knew that this would involve suffering and death, because he loved the world. Christians believe that although Jesus suffered and died on the cross, he had done nothing wrong to deserve this.

According to Christian teaching, Jesus sacrificed his own life for the rest of the world, and took the punishment that everyone deserves because they fail to do what God wants. This sacrifice made it possible for people to be forgiven for the wrong things they do (their sins). Instead of being punished after death, they can now have eternal life with God if they believe in Jesus. Christians often talk about 'salvation' and about 'being saved'. They mean that they believe the death of Jesus saved them from the consequences of sin and gave them the opportunity of heaven.

John's Gospel puts it like this:

> *For God so loved the world that he gave his one and only Son, that whoever believes in him shall not perish but have eternal life.*
>
> *(John 3:16)*

Christians believe that the death of Jesus on the cross was a sacrifice which gives everyone the opportunity of eternal life with God.

Christianity is not just about believing, but is also about doing. There is not much point in having beliefs if they don't make any difference to the way you think or behave.

Christians have all different ways of putting their faith into action. Most think that it is very important to care for other people, particularly those who are poor, weak, old or ill. Some Christians regularly visit people in hospital, or people who are in prison, or elderly people who can't get out of the house very easily. Some run pre-school playgroups, or do shopping and washing for disabled neighbours, or volunteer to help organisations such as the *Samaritans* or *Amnesty International*. Sometimes, Christians help in charity shops, or serve meals for the homeless in the winter. Many Christians try to do at least something in their local community to help other people.

Christians usually try to give money on a regular basis to people who have less than they do. Some work for aid agencies such as *CAFOD*,

STOP & Think ?

➤ Do you, or any members of your family, do any kind of voluntary work? Why, or why not?

Tearfund or *Christian Aid*, which help people in developing countries who have no clean water or whose lives have been disrupted by war, famine or disaster. Christians who don't work for aid agencies still try to help, by making donations and taking part in fund-raising activities. Some Christian churches send volunteers to countries such as Romania, where they deliver parcels of donated medicines and clothing to people who have very little.

Christians believe that it's important to put their faith into action by caring for other people. The photo shows a volunteer helping at a Christmas dinner for the homeless.

What do you know?

❶ What does the word 'Messiah' mean?

❷ What do Christians mean when they talk about the 'Incarnation'?

❸ What do Jews believe will happen before the Messiah comes to the world?

❹ **a.** Why did Mary and Joseph go to Bethlehem just before Jesus was born?

b. Who were the first people to come and visit the baby Jesus?

c. What were the three gifts that the Magi gave to Jesus?

❺ What sort of things did Jesus teach people about?

❻ Give three examples of miracles Jesus is said to have performed.

❼ How did Jesus die?

❽ What do Christians mean when they say that the death of Jesus 'saved' them?

❾ Why do some Christians support the work of overseas aid agencies?

❿ What might Christians do to put their faith into action in their local communities?

What do you think?

❶ Some people think that Christmas should only be celebrated by Christians, because otherwise it becomes too greedy and the message is lost. What do you think?

❷ Sometimes people say that they agree with Jesus' teaching, but that they can't believe in the miracle stories because they are just too unlikely. Do you agree with this point of view? Give reasons for your answer.

action INTO

❶ In Christian art, there are many examples of paintings that illustrate the birth of Jesus. Using the Internet or books, find out about some of them, and choose one or two that you particularly like. Write an explanation to go with the picture. What is the main focus of the picture? What does the artist seem to be saying about Jesus? You might put 'Nativity' into a search, or try: http://www.nationalgallery.org.uk

❷ Find out about how one of the following organisations has tried to put Christian beliefs into action:

• Christian Aid
• Salvation Army
• CAFOD
• Tearfund

Make an advertising leaflet to encourage Christians to support the organisation you have chosen. Explain what it does and how this fits in with Christian beliefs.

❸ Do some research to find out more about the work of a famous Christian. You might choose: Mother Teresa of Calcutta; Elizabeth Fry; Martin Luther King; Dr Barnardo. What did this person do? Why did they do it?

❹ What kinds of voluntary work do you think are needed in your local community? Design an advertisement for display in a church, to encourage Christians to volunteer.

❺ Conduct a survey to find out why people celebrate Christmas. See how many celebrate it for religious reasons, and how many for other reasons such as tradition or the chance to see family and friends. Present your results as a chart with a key.

Why is prayer an important part of life for so many people?

The Big Picture

In this unit you will learn:

- what is meant by prayer
- why people pray
- how people feel that prayer helps them
- the particular importance of prayer to Christians and Muslims.

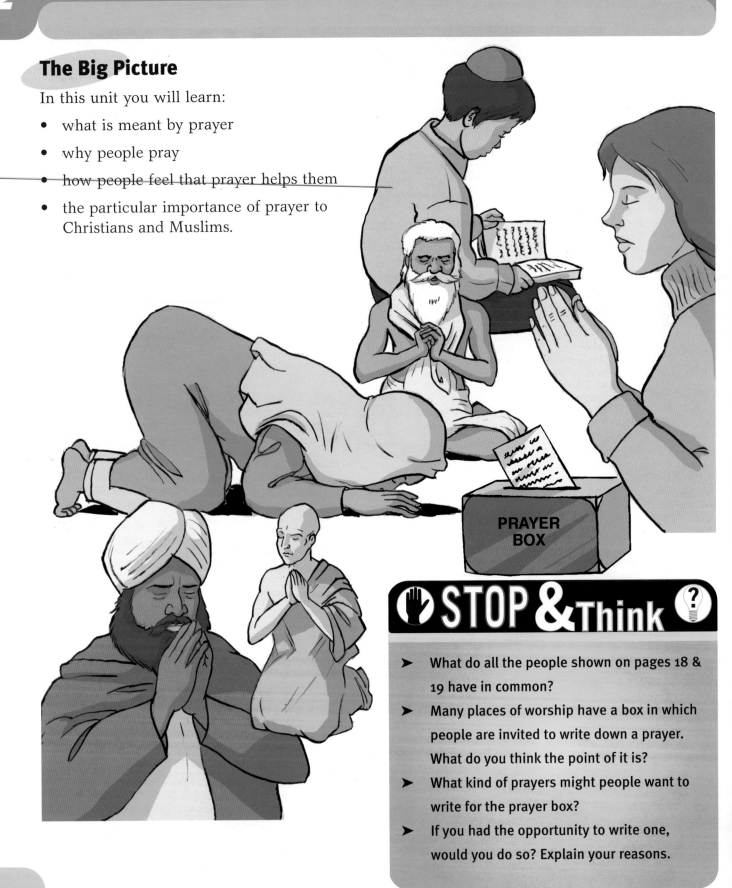

PRAYER BOX

STOP & Think

➤ What do all the people shown on pages 18 & 19 have in common?

➤ Many places of worship have a box in which people are invited to write down a prayer. What do you think the point of it is?

➤ What kind of prayers might people want to write for the prayer box?

➤ If you had the opportunity to write one, would you do so? Explain your reasons.

The poem below reflects the variety of prayer. It is called *The Sense of Divine* which means 'the awareness of God'.

The Sense of Divine

Driven by conscience
Or a duty that calls;
Communing with nature
Or inside holy walls.
Candles, incense, adoration;
Alone in quiet meditation.
In hope or thanksgiving,
In dark and despair.
Five times a day;
Every week;
Once a year.
In lofty cathedrals,
With prayer book and beads;
Hands held together confessing wrong deeds.
Barefoot in mosque, body bowed deep,
Chanting that prayer is better than sleep.
Speaking in union, together in thought,
Inspired by the words that others have taught.
Over the graveside;
At home by the shrine;
Aware of a presence –
The sense of divine.

text message.........

People who believe in God look upon prayer as an important part of their faith. Prayer is their way of communicating with God and an essential part of their lives. Buddhists, who do not believe in God, use meditation (which is similar to prayer) to communicate with their inner selves. There are many different ways of praying and reasons for doing so. Some prayer takes place at places of worship when people of a particular faith meet together. On these occasions, there will often be prayers based on teachings from sacred writings, which are recited or read from a prayer book. Most religions teach that it is also important to pray privately. Although there may be set times for this, it is also believed that God can be prayed to at any time and in individual ways. Reasons for prayer include showing thanks, saying sorry and asking for something for oneself or other people.

Look at the following prayers

Oh God, help those in power to make the right decisions so that all people might live in peace.

Please God make the things I've revised come up in the exams.

Give me strength to face li without him.

Make him stop bullying me.

Forgive me for bullying. Help me think before I say hurtful things.

Thank you for the joy of today.

STOP & Think ?

➤ Why might a person prefer to pray on their own?

➤ When might they want to pray with other people?

➤ Where would you most like to be if you were praying or meditating? Give your reasons.

❚❚ PAUSE & RECORD

• Which of the prayers shown above, do you think it would be right for believers to expect God to listen to? Give your reasons.

• Make up six more examples of things people might pray for; three which you consider are *right* to pray for, and three which are not.

Like all people of faith, Christians consider prayer to be an important part of their lives.

Britney Spears: "I keep a prayer journal and I write in it every night."

➤ What value could there be in keeping a prayer journal? How do you think it would be used?

➤ Why do you think that confession (admitting to the wrong things you have done) and asking for forgiveness is an important part of prayer?

➤ How do you feel when you have done something wrong? What do you do about it?

Declan Donnelly, from the Ant and Dec partnership is a Roman Catholic Christian who attends Mass where he regularly goes to confession. Although he prefers to be private about his faith he thinks there is no harm in publicly thanking God. "We have both been so lucky."

23

text message.........

Although for Christians, prayer can take place anywhere and at any time, it will be an important part of their worship when they go to church. Here they will often follow a set pattern of prayers, spoken aloud by the whole congregation. They will usually end their prayers with the word amen, 'may it be so'.

This is what will usually be included when a Christian prays:

Praise or adoration – showing love to God

Repentance or confession – being sorry and asking God's forgiveness

Asking or petitioning – requesting something on behalf of other people

Your own needs – asking something for oneself

Saying thank you – showing gratitude

✋ STOP & Think ❓

➤ How might
a) the lighting of a candle, and
b) studying an icon (image of Jesus or special holy person connected with him) help people when they pray?

Not just in church

Children brought up in Christian families are usually encouraged to pray at home. Sometimes this will involve family prayers, which can range from a short prayer called *grace* said before or after a meal, to prayers for special occasions, including important festival times such as Easter or the anniversary of a family member. Young children especially are taught to pray at key times, often at bedtime.

The following extract is about a young orphan girl called Anne. She has been brought up in an orphanage and has now been sent to stay with a middle-aged Christian couple.

MARILLA: Say your prayers now and get into bed.

ANNE: I never say any prayers.

MARILLA: You must say your prayers while you are under my roof, Anne.

ANNE: Why of course, if you want me to. After I get into bed I'll imagine a real nice prayer.

MARILLA: You must kneel down.

ANNE: Why must people kneel down to pray? If I really wanted to pray, I'll tell you what I'd do. I'd go out into a great big field all alone or into the deep, deep woods, and I'd look up into that lovely blue sky that looks as if there was no end to its blueness. And then I'd FEEL a prayer.

From 'Anne of Green Gables' by L.M. Montgomery.

- Write down one reason why Christians see a value in learning and using set prayers, and one value of individual, made-up prayers.
- Study the pictures in this unit and write down your thoughts and impressions on how you think people are feeling when they pray.

STOP & Think

➤ Why do you think some people think it right to kneel down when they pray?

➤ What do you think Anne meant be saying she would *feel* a prayer?

➤ What kind of things might she feel in the places she described?

Jesus plays a very important part in Christian prayer. They believe that they can pray to God through him. He showed them how.

By his own example

Asking God for strength and courage

'My Father, if it is possible, take this cup of suffering from me! Yet not what I want, but what you want.' *Matthew 26:39*

Asking for others to be forgiven

'Forgive them, Father! They don't know what they are doing.' *Luke 23:34*

By his teaching

Be sincere

'When you pray, do not use a lot of meaningless words...'

Matthew 6:7

Pray alone

'But when you pray, go to your room, close the door, and pray to your Father, who is unseen.'

Matthew 6:6

Pray together

'Whenever two of you on earth agree about anything you pray for, it will be done for you by my Father in heaven. For where two or three come together in my name, I am there with them.'

Matthew 18:20

Ask for the right things

The words below have come to be known as The Lord's Prayer.

*'Our father in heaven:
May your holy name be honoured;
may your kingdom come;
may your will be done on earth as it is in heaven.
Give us today the food we need.
Forgive us the wrongs we have done,
as we forgive the wrongs that others have done to us.
Do not bring us to hard testing, but keep us safe from the Evil One.'*

Matthew 6:9–13.

The Lord's Prayer in text:

Dad@hvn, ur spshl.we want wot u want&urth2b like hvn.giv us food&4giv r sins lyk we 4giv uvaz.don't test us! saveus! Bcos we kno ur boss, ur tuf&ur cool 4eva! ok?

- Write your own version of The Lord's Prayer that you think would be suitable for a Christian child learning it for the first time.

27

text message.........

For Muslims, prayer is a direct way of communicating with ALLAH (God). It can be performed both alone and with other people. Muslims have five special duties known as the Five Pillars of Islam. The second of these pillars is called SALAH. This is a formal act of worship in which Muslims show their obedience to Allah by praying five times a day; before sunrise, midday, mid-afternoon, early evening and late evening. Salah can be performed at any clean place and Muslims will often pray at home as well as at work or school. On Fridays, a special day for Muslims, many go to the masjid (mosque) for the noon-day prayers known as the JUMU'AH.

There are certain requirements for performing salah.

When Muslims pray they must:

- prepare by performing **WUDU** (washing hands, face and feet)

- wear clean clothes

- find a clean place, often using a prayer mat

- face the direction of the **KA'BAH** (the central part of the grand mosque) in Makkah

- have the right intentions

- speak the prayers aloud, accompanying each with a set of special movements known as a **RAK'AH**.

Not just a duty

Although salah is one of the duties a Muslim is expected to carry out, it is seen as more than that. It is considered to be a way of 'refreshing' the believer. The benefits of prayer can be seen in the following extract:

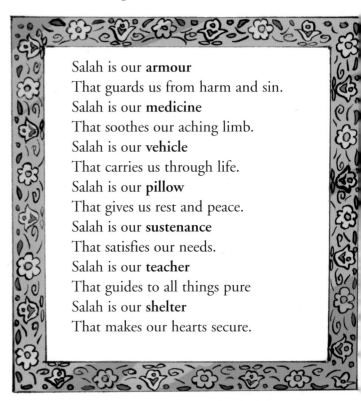

Salah is our **armour**
That guards us from harm and sin.
Salah is our **medicine**
That soothes our aching limb.
Salah is our **vehicle**
That carries us through life.
Salah is our **pillow**
That gives us rest and peace.
Salah is our **sustenance**
That satisfies our needs.
Salah is our **teacher**
That guides to all things pure
Salah is our **shelter**
That makes our hearts secure.

STOP &Think ?

➤ What do you think a Muslim would see as the value of praying at intervals through the day?

➤ What might be a difficulty in performing Salah correctly?

➤ The poem describes the benefits of prayer by using several similes (comparisons). Can you think of any other similes that might be used by Muslims in the same way?

- Write in your books the words written in capitals on pages 28 and 29. Underneath each one, write a sentence of explanation.

In addition to salah, many Muslims pray in their own private way. Such prayer, known as **DU'A**, does not have a set pattern and can take place anywhere and at any time. Sometimes a string of 99 prayer beads is used (usually in three sets of 33). This is known as a **SUBHAH** and it reminds Muslims of the 99 names of Allah referred to in the **QUR'AN**, the most holy book in Islam. These names are words that describe the attributes (qualities) of Allah and concentrating on them helps Muslims to feel closer to him.

The verses below, taken from the Qur'an, give Muslims two important teachings about prayer:

Allah alone should be praised as the one true God.

> 'All praise is for Allah, the Lord of the Universe, the most kind, Master of the Day of Judgement. You alone we worship, from you alone we seek help.'
>
> *(Surah 1:1–7)*

Prayers should have the right intentions and be matched by right actions.

> 'Woe to the praying ones who are unmindful of their prayers, who pray to be seen, and who withhold alms [charity].'
>
> *(Surah 107:4–7)*

Some of the names of Allah:

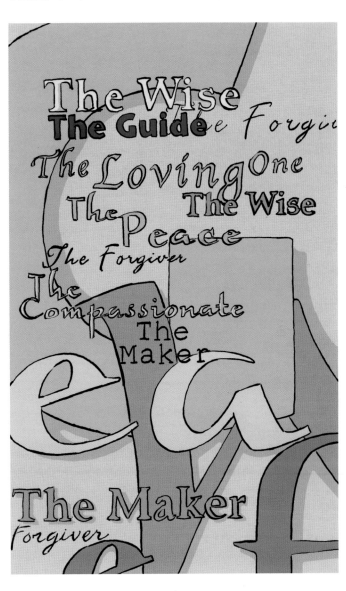

Abu Talha's Garden

Abu Talha had a beautiful garden through which a stream of sparkling, clear water flowed. Abu Talha loved to say his prayers in this garden. Over his head the palm trees would sway, and he would thank Allah for all the goodness he had been shown.

One hot, sleepy afternoon, Abu set out into his garden with his prayer mat. He could hear the stream gurgling and the palm trees swaying as he started his prayers, when suddenly he stopped. He heard a lovely, high-pitched chirping from the tree above him. Abu opened his eyes and looked up, and there above him was the most beautiful bird with bright plumage, long flowing tail feathers and a lovely song. He was fascinated, and stopped to look for a few moments, but was then ashamed for he was supposed to be praying. So he continued his prayers.

The next day, Abu was again in the garden praying. The bird appeared once more, but this time it was building a nest. As it built, it sang and chirped beautifully above Abu's head. Abu watched the bird. He did not know where he was in his prayers and was unable to concentrate. Then he felt ashamed. He thought, 'How can my prayers reach Allah if I get muddled and lose concentration?' He knew that a good Muslim should say prayers properly and think only of Allah during worship.

So Abu went to the Prophet Muhammad. 'My head is full of my garden, the stream, the swaying palms and the beautiful bird,' he said, 'and they are stopping me from worshipping Allah. Take my gardens and use them for all the Muslims in Madina.' The Prophet accepted the gift, and Abu Talha, from then on, was able to pray to Allah without any distractions.

STOP & Think

➤ What else might help people concentrate and not be distracted when they pray?

➤ Some people might think the opposite to Abu and feel that the garden was a good place to pray. What reason might they give?

PAUSE & RECORD

- Write in your books three different things a Muslim might want to pray about. In each case, choose one of the names on page 29 which would be the most suitable aspect of Allah to focus upon.

Example:

Praying for personal strength to be more thoughtful to people who are lonely and unhappy. Name of Allah: *The Compassionate* (meaning sympathetic).

be used by anyone. Those believing in God can put the thought to him. Those who don't believe in God can make it an inner resolution to themselves.

A Thought Prayer

Let there be peace on earth
and let it begin with me.

Let there be love on earth
and let it begin in my heart.

Let there be a future
and let it begin with my action – now.

Prayer is an activity that often unites people. Many places of work are now building prayer rooms where people of all religions can go and pray in their own way. In airports in Britain there is a prayer room where people of any faith may go and worship.

Shared prayers

Often in times of great sadness, people of different faiths come together and share prayers. One of the prayers used on such occasions has come to be known as **The International Prayer for Peace**.

Lead me from death to life, from falsehood to truth.
Lead me from despair to hope, from fear to trust.
Lead me from hate to love, from war to peace.
Let peace fill our heart, our world our universe.

People who do not believe in God, such as Buddhists and those without any religious faith, also feel the need to think deeply about many of the same things as those praying to God. This is usually known as meditation. It is sometimes called a 'Thought Prayer'. This can

✋STOP &Think❓

➤ Why do you think people of different faiths come together to pray in times of sadness?
➤ Do you know about any other times when they might join in prayer?

Using pages 18–31 to help you, work through the following questions and activities:

What do you know?

❶ Name four aids to prayer, two Christian and two Muslim. Give an explanation for each one.

❷ The following statements are all wrong. Rewrite the words written in bold, giving them the correct meanings.

> **Repentance** means asking something for oneself.

> **Adoration** means asking God's forgiveness.

> **Petitioning** means being sorry.

> **Confession** means showing gratitude.

> **Praise** means asking something on behalf of other people.

❸ Explain the differences between **salah** and **du'a**.

❹ Write a paragraph for a magazine explaining the importance of prayer to *either* Muslims *or* Christians.

What do you think?

❶ Write a letter to the headteacher of a school that does not have a prayer room, giving reasons why it would be a good idea to have one.

❷ Some people say that 'prayer refreshes the parts of that nothing else reaches.' How do you think this could be?

❸ For homework, find three people of different ages who pray, and ask them the questions below. Try to discover the reasons for their answers.

• Do you prefer to pray on your own or with other people?

• Do you prefer to make up your own prayer or use a set prayer?

action INTO

❶ One of the pictures on page 20 shows a prayer box. Design a prayer box or prayer board that you think would be in keeping with the feelings associated with prayer, using appropriate pictures or symbols.

❷ Read the Muslim poem on page 28. Choose three of the words written in bold and illustrate what you think the meaning of the word would look like. Example: **shelter** picture of a cosy house during a storm.

❸ Decide upon an important occasion for a whole school assembly and make up a Thought Prayer for it, which would be suitable for pupils of any or no faith.

❹ Read the scene below which takes place during World War II. It is between a young woman called Carrie, who is desperate for the safe return of her boyfriend, and her mother who is a trying to calm her down and comfort her. Write or act out how the conversation might continue.

Carrie: (crying) I can't bear it, not knowing. Every time I hear fresh news of the bombing I fear the worst.

MOTHER: There, there, steady on now. You've just got to have faith and keep praying, Carrie.

CARRIE: I don't believe God's listening, why else would he let all these terrible things happen? Anyway, what about the people in Germany? They're probably praying to God too.

MOTHER: God didn't make the war Carrie, people did. Prayer isn't going to win the war but I honestly believe praying can help in other ways.

CARRIE: Such as?

Final Thoughts

This unit has asked: What is prayer? You have learned that prayer is important to people of all faiths. Taking at least half a page in your book, write down your responses to the following:

• Some interesting facts I didn't know before.

• Why I pray *or* Why I don't pray.

• Questions about prayer that I would like to ask a believer in God.

• Aspects of prayer which I'd like to explore further.

Dig deep in your pockets!

Almost everyone's given to charity at some point. Some people drop money in a rattled can when they're out shopping. Other people give a certain amount every month. Some people give lots, others a little. Some don't give anything at all. Some feel good about it, some would like to avoid it. Some feel guilty, others feel pleased with themselves.

This section will look at the following questions:

- What is charity?

- Why do we give to charity (or not)?

- How do we give and what's done with our money?

- What do world religions have to say about giving to charity?

Pi$$a madness?

Tom Monaghan made his fortune in pizzas. His Domino's Pizza empire stretches all over the world. But although he was fabulously wealthy he was troubled. There seemed to him to be something wrong with him having so much money while others had so little. His solution was simple. He didn't really need all that money, and other people could benefit from it so... in 1998 he sold most of his share in Domino's Pizza. Out of the sale he made around $1billion. He will give this away gradually to charities related to Catholic Christianity. He says he wants to 'die broke'. This is because he takes the Bible teaching seriously which says 'It is easier for a camel to pass through the eye of a needle than for a rich man to enter God's Kingdom'.

PAUSE & RECORD

- Do you think Tom is right to give away his money? Discuss this in groups and come up with some arguments for and against his actions.

Back to basics

People have always helped each other. We share things. We give things away when we've got too much (or we don't want them any more). We help those who aren't as lucky as us. That's charity. Sometimes we give money, sometimes we give our time, sometimes we give things directly which belong to us.

In Britain, organised charity really took off with the religious orders in the middle ages. Monks and nuns helped people whose lives were hard. They didn't ask for anything in return.

Another big 'boost' for charity came during the industrial revolution. Factories were dirty, dangerous and took advantage of their workers. They sometimes made orphan children work in terrible conditions. Some believed this was wrong. They set about changing it. But they knew that it wasn't enough just to give the poor money, they had to help them improve their lives for themselves. Many organised charities began at this time.

Houses built for the poor

Charity never ends

Today, there are still child-slaves in the world.

Not long ago, some children in Africa were freed from slavery. Their parents had sold them for about $5. There are still children who work long hours in dangerous jobs. There are still millions of people dying every year of starvation. Yet there are many hundreds of charities and many millions of people who give money and help them in other ways.

Should it be our duty to give to charity, or should we choose to do it freely? Should you give quietly or be open about it? Does it matter how much or how little we give? What's the best way to give? Who or what deserves to

✋ STOP & Think ❓

➤ Discuss the questions in groups. Make a list of some of the points raised and write them on a flipchart.
How much do you give to charity at the moment? How often? Which charities? Could you do more? Should you do more? Why do you give? (or why don't you?) Are some charities more worthy than others?

Whose responsibility?

Eric and Karen are two senior students in an ordinary comprehensive school.

ERIC: There's only one thing that bothers me about giving to charity.

KAREN: Yeah, what's that?

ERIC: It just means the government can avoid their own responsibilities.

KAREN: How come?

ERIC: Well, look at our school. How many times have we had to raise money for trips, musical instruments... books.

KAREN: I know, get's right in the way of schoolwork sometimes.

ERIC: So, I mean the government should pay for all this stuff. That's why our parents pay their taxes after all.

KAREN: My mum's a nurse. Her hospital's always having to do the same thing. You'd think they would have better things to do.

ERIC: Yeah, so isn't it also the government's responsibility to help the homeless and feed the hungry? If I give to charity, I'm just doing their job for them.

KAREN: True... but if we didn't then lots more people would suffer. I suppose the government can't do everything.

ERIC: Why not?

Why give?

Most people agree that it's right to give to charity. They agree that this is part of being human and helping others who need help. But maybe whether we give to charity or not (and how much we give) depends on our reasons behind giving. Thinking about these reasons should help us examine whether we could (or should) help more. The following are some reasons why people might give to charity.

It makes me feel better

Everyone knows the story of Ebenezer Scrooge. He eventually becomes a kind-hearted old man at Christmas because he is shown some uncomfortable things. He's shown how poor his relatives are. He's shown how miserable he has become since he got rich. But it's not until he's shown his own funeral that he really gets going. No one cares that he's died. He decides he doesn't want that – he wants people to care about him. So, he starts splashing his money about. Maybe giving to charity is a way of making ourselves feel better, or making others feel good about us.

It stops me feeling guilty

Some people know how lucky they are. They know how unlucky others are. Helping out makes us feel less guilty about our own good lives.

I don't want to be seen as mean

Sometimes we give because we want to be like others. If all your friends chuck a coin in a collecting can, you might feel pressure to do the same. Otherwise they might think badly of you.

I hope someone would do the same for me

Some people give because they identify with a problem. They imagine themselves in the same situation. They hope that if they were ever like that, someone would help them. So they help. Sometimes this works 'backwards'. For example, if you'd been adopted as a child you might be more likely to give to charities which help children in care.

It helps me feel less attached to wealth

Some people believe that wealth can 'blind you' to life's problems. You can become too attached to money. It stresses you out trying to hold on to it. If you give it away this problem goes away. Many of the world's religions have this view. Some say that having too much money becomes a burden. If you give it away, you make your burden lighter.

It'll make the world a better place

Some people give to charity just because they think it'll make things better. Poverty and hardship in the world can't be good. They must cause problems somehow. Maybe if people are poor it makes the world less secure. If you're poor you might do some strange things to help yourself. You might be forced to take things from others, or take part in wars. This makes the world less safe for everyone. There's nothing more dangerous than someone who thinks they've nothing to lose. So helping people improve their lives must be better for everyone.

It'll eventually be good for me

A fair world, where everyone feels valued, where everyone has enough to eat, where no one suffers because they are poor or disadvantaged, where people can live life to the fullest whatever their circumstances; that has to be good for us all one way or another. Maybe giving to charity is good because it will somehow reward the giver eventually.

✋STOP &Think ❓

➤ Do you think there are 'good' and 'bad' reasons for giving to charity? Or does it matter why you give at all?

PAUSE & RECORD

- Before you read this section discuss in groups the different ways people might give to charity. See which group can come up with most.

'Knee-jerk'

- You're watching the TV and see pictures of starving people. You want to help so you write a cheque.

- It's Christmas. You're feeling generous. The charities are out in force. So you give.

- There's a situation such as an earthquake – a direct need. So you help.

- There's a special event. You want to feel part of it. You pledge some money.

- A problem is identified. Popstars sing a song. You buy the song – so you help the cause.

The only problem with this approach is that people easily forget that the problems are still there, even once the special day or event has come and gone.

Sustained giving

Some people give to charity more regularly. There are various ways of doing this:

- You can join an organisation which costs a certain amount a year. For this you get newsletters and reports. Some of your money goes to help others. You might pay a monthly fee to the charity. This comes straight out of your bank account. Sometimes this goes to a charity to be used generally. Other times it might go to something more specific. For example, some people 'adopt' children in developing countries. They pay money each month to help support the child as he or she grows up. There's even 'adopt a granny' schemes doing the same for elderly people.

- In Britain there's also a system called Give As You Earn. Here, money comes off your wages before you even get them. It goes straight to the charity.

- Some people give a percentage of their income every year or month. Religions often encourage this approach.

- Some people might just decide that each year/month/day they'll give a certain amount of money to charity.

The Lottery problem

Some years ago, Britain started a National Lottery. This is very popular, but it raises some important questions about charity and giving. Every pound spent on a National Lottery ticket helps charity, but:

1 Since the Lottery began, charities have complained that the amount of money they make has decreased. People seem to prefer to give to charity when it also means they might become millionaires! Instead of giving to charities people are using their money to buy Lottery tickets.

2 Some people also criticise the amount of money which goes to charity from the Lottery. Only a small part of each one-pound ticket is actually used for charitable work.

3 The Lottery organisation is there to make a profit too, which charities do not try to do. Is it right for a private company to make money out of people giving to charity?

4 Some complain about the kinds of things lottery money has been used for. Some feel that supporting things like opera and theatre is not as important as helping the poor and feeding the hungry. They feel that lottery money should be allocated more fairly.

5 Some people worry about who is buying Lottery tickets. The Lottery has been called a 'tax on the poor'. This is because the poorer you are the more attractive a Lottery win is. So, you spend too much on Lottery tickets, making you even poorer. The chances of winning are so low that this doesn't make sense.

6 The only people who benefit are the winners. Maybe the Lottery should have more prizes of less money. At least this way, more people will actually benefit, instead of making a very small number of people very rich.

7 There was an attempt recently to start up a 'people's lottery', where more of the money raised would actually go to needy causes. This was unsuccessful.

Many people think the lottery is great. It raises lots of money for good causes... and it gives you the chance to become rich!!

action INTO

Have a class debate.

'Should the Lottery be banned?'.

All in a good cause

There are thousands of charities. Some big, some small. Some at home, others abroad. They deal with all sorts of problems and issues. Some raise money, others take in goods and give them to those who need them. Some ask for your time, others ask you to write letters or march in the streets. All have at least two things in common.

- They are trying to **re-distribute wealth and privilege** from those who have it to those who don't.

AND/OR

- They are trying to make life better.

Here are some examples of different kinds of charities.

Poverty relief

OXFAM is a non-religious organisation which tries to help the poor at home and abroad. It runs shops which sell Fair Trade goods, as well as second–hand items. It works on the idea that the rich here in Britain can use their wealth and purchasing power to make a difference. It sends direct aid where it's needed, either in the form of financial help, or in goods and services. It tries to help the poor get back on their own feet and take control of their own lives.

Social Justice

The Big Issue is sold on the streets. Sellers are homeless people. For every issue sold they make money. But the magazine also helps people to think about the issue of homelessness and so tries to make them do something about it – even if it's only writing a letter to their MP.

Turning lives around

The Bethany Trust works with drug rehabilitation in Edinburgh. It tries to help addicts come off drugs, find a job and get their lives back on track. Cafes and shelters are provided, as well as practical help and counselling.

Making life easier

Down's Syndrome Scotland helps people with this condition. It helps their families too. It helps people with Down's Syndrome to learn useful skills. It also helps educate others about Down's Syndrome, and so hopefully, help fight against any prejudices which people might have.

Giving kids a purpose

Livingston Aquanauts Swimming Club raises money through raffles, bag-packing and other events. It gives young people the opportunity to do well at something. It also trains them in important skills like teamwork, loyalty, hard work and commitment.

What is
DOWN'S SYNDROME?

Information for parents, carers, professionals and students

Down's Syndrome

PAUSE & RECORD

- Here are some symbols/logos for charities. In groups discuss the following;
  What does the symbol tell you about the charity? Do some research on the internet on some of the charities.

action INTO

Working in groups, choose an issue you feel strongly about. Now devise a new charity organisation which could respond to that issue. Think about the following:

- What will your charity do?
- How will it raise money?
- What will its logo/symbol look like?
- How will the charity be organised?

You should present your ideas to the rest of the class.

Love one another

Most Christians agree that this is one of Jesus' most important teachings (Matthew 22:34–40) You can pick and choose bits of the Bible to support lots of ideas – sometimes even completely opposite points of view! But this thread runs through all Jesus' teaching. Some Christians would say that Jesus taught more about this than about anything else. In practice, loving others means you should help anyone in need. You can do this by giving to charity. The very first Christians agreed to share their wealth out (Acts 2:34–35). Some at the time believed that being wealthy was a blessing from God (and so being poor was God's punishment). But many also just saw poverty and injustice as something to be fixed. God gave some wealth which they should use to help others.

Jesus also taught that we should give to charity without making a big show of it (Matthew 6:2–4). He said that the reward for helping others will come from God.

Jesus also said that wealth could become too important to you. You might end up only caring about wealth and nothing else. Giving it away not only helps others, but it also 'builds up riches' for you in heaven.

Jesus did say to one rich young man that he would never enter the Kingdom of God until he'd given *everything* away. (Matthew 19:16–22).

➤ What examples can you think of where Christians help others?

Teaching from the Bible

As Jesus sat near the Temple treasury, he watched the people as they dropped in their money. Many rich men dropped in a lot of money; then a poor widow came along and dropped in two little copper coins worth about a penny. Jesus called his disciples together and said to them, 'I tell you that this poor widow put more in the offering box than all the others. For the others put in what they had to spare of their riches; but she, poor as she is, put in all she had – she gave all she had to live on.

Mark 12:41–44, Good News Bible

Meaning: Jesus meant that it wasn't important how much you actually give. But you should give as much as you can. The widow's coins were 'worth' much more than the rich people's money because they were a much larger part of what she had. They just gave what they had left over. She gave all she had. So for modern Christians it's not enough just to give what you've got left after you've spent what you want. You should give first then live off what's left.

Forms of giving

Christians give in very different ways:

* Tithing: Some give a percentage of their yearly income to charity. They give this before they spend anything.

- Vows of poverty: When Christians become members of religious orders, they often hand over everything they own. This is then shared among the needy.

- Regular collections: Most Christian churches take a weekly collection during their service. This is a response to hearing God's word. Some of this money will go to charity.

- Special situations: Christians don't just give money. Giving to charity can also be goods. It can also be time given to help the needy. Many churches support particular charities or respond to crises as they happen.

Real Christians

Nicky Nicholls works for Christian Aid. She does lots of different things, as she explains:

'One day I'm reading heavy texts on debt cancellation, the next day I'm interviewing a clown! . . . One reason people like me want to be in the Church is to make a difference in the wider world. I believe that everyone has the right to life in all its fullness . . . If you follow Jesus you can't be inward-looking, though churches sometimes seem more worried about pews and fonts than poverty and hunger'.

From RE Today Autumn 2001 page 31.

Christian charity in action

The Salvation Army is one of the best-known examples of a Christian Charity. It calls itself 'Christianity with its sleeves rolled up'. It runs hostels for the homeless; drug rehabilitation centres; children's homes; hostels for the poor; food distribution centres, and many other examples of charitable actions. All its money comes from what people give it. It is now one of the biggest helping agencies in the world.

Special times, special giving

Harvest – each year Christians celebrate God's care for people by celebrating the harvest. Usually at this time, foods brought to churches are given away to the needy.

Christmas – God sent his son for everyone. We should be grateful and should show this by helping others.

Maundy Thursday – The Thursday before Easter is a time when Christians show their love for others by doing charitable acts.

Many Christians also give money to charity when celebrating special events in their lives, like the Baptism of a child.

An opportunity

In the Islamic world a beggar on the street isn't a pest to be ignored. He's a chance to show mercy, love and compassion. Muslims believe that charity isn't something you just choose to do – it's something you must do. Allah values each human and cares for everyone, but he expects us to look after each other too.

Muslims believe that all Islam is a brotherhood (Ummah). This means that everyone is responsible for everyone else. If someone's life is hard, then we should share the task of caring for him and making his life better. This is not just a way of being kind, it's a way of thanking Allah. It's a way of showing our gratitude for the good things in our lives.

In this way, it's also a way of worshipping Allah. This is called sadaqah.

Charity is so important in Islam that it is one of the five pillars. These are ideas that the whole faith is based on. Every Muslim should keep the five pillars. Each one is a duty, not a choice. Zakat is one of these pillars. It means giving to charity generally as well as giving a part of your yearly income to the needy. It works like this:

Each year you earn a certain amount of money. You take from this money what you need. You need to pay your bills, feed your family and that kind of thing. You then take what you have left and give 2.5% of it away. This money is used to help the needy. The rest is yours.

Muslims believe that Zakat has many uses:

- It helps those in need.
- It reminds you that you depend on the grace of Allah too.
- It's a way of thanking Allah for your life.
- It helps you be less attached to your wealth. You can then be more interested in your religious life.

This doesn't mean that you won't give more than this amount to charity each year. But this is the minimum. It is something you must do – if you want to call yourself a Muslim.

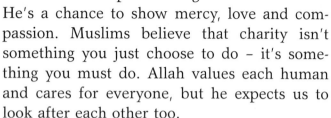

> ➤ **Do you think Zakat is a helpful thing for Muslims, or is it a pain?**

Teaching from the Qur'an

You shall not attain righteousness unless you spend on others that which you love, and whatever you spend truly Allah knows.

Surah 3:92

Meaning: You will only improve your life spiritually if you help others. You can do this by giving to charity. Allah sees everything, and knows everything. So he will know how much you have helped – or haven't!

Other forms of charity

Muslims also help the needy in other ways. For example, many British Muslims are proud that there aren't many old Muslim people in care. Muslims believe that it's their responsibility to help those in need in their community. So if someone has no family to look after them, another Muslim family may take them in. Also, Muhammed allowed men to have more than one wife – as long as he could afford to look after each one equally. In Muhammed's time this was a way of looking after women whose husbands had died.

Real Muslims

Arshad is a Muslim teenager. He already gives Zakat – from his paper round! He believes that it's right to do this:

> 'If I take my religion seriously I should perform its duties whether I like them or not. A part of me wouldn't mind hanging on to that 2.5%! Like any teenager I like spending. But I think that this money is something I should be grateful for. I can show I'm grateful by sharing some of it with others. This makes their lives better. Even though I'm young, I'll still have to stand before Allah one day. He'll judge me. I want him to think highly of me. That's a lot more important to me than the CDs I could have spent that money on!!'

Islamic charity in action

Islamic Relief is a charity run by Muslims. It tries to help those in need. It also wants to challenge the causes of need. The first ever donation Islamic Relief got was 20p from a 12 year-old. It now runs projects in more than 22 countries.

Special times, special giving

Birth of a baby – Soon after a Muslim baby is born its head is shaved. This is an event for the whole family. The hair which comes off is weighed. The weight in gold is given to the poor.

Ramadan and Eid – After sunset every day during Ramadan, Muslims will break their special fast. Often, the poor and needy will be invited to share this meal. This also happens at the end of Ramadan during the festival of Eid-al-fitr.

The Hajj – At Eid ul Adha, during the Hajj, many animals are sacrificed. The meat from these animals is usually given to the poor.

Goats that are to be sacrificed.

- Can you see any similarities between 'special times' in Islam and Christianity?

3

Charity = righteousness

Jews believe that the world needs to be healed. It is full of greed, unfairness, poverty. This is because people aren't in the right relationship with God. God created everything to be perfect, but humans spoiled it by turning away from him. Jews believe they are 'or lagoyim' – a light to the nations. It is the special responsibility of followers of Judaism to set good examples for the rest of the world to follow. One of the best ways of showing others what's right is by helping those in need. This is called tzedaka, which means charity, but also means righteousness! (Deuteronomy 15:7–8). Showing others how to live properly will help people turn back to God. Then the world will be perfect again.

The Jewish prophets spoke out against unfairness. They taught that it was everyone's responsibility to help the needy. They complained about people being kept in poverty, and about rich people thinking they were special. They said that the way we treat others should be the same way God treats us – with love, care and kindness. Jews believe that giving to others is a way of giving back to God.

The Ten Commandments are the basics of Jewish belief about how to live. Seven are about how we treat each other.

Jews think its just as important to help non-Jews by charitable actions. Their own history reminds them that they were once an unloved and unwanted group of people (Leviticus 22:20).

STOP & Think ?

➤ From what you know about Judaism already, can you think of two times in history when Jewish people would have felt, 'unloved and unwanted'?

Teaching from the Jewish scriptures

If you refuse to listen to the cry of the poor, your own cry for help will not be heard.

Prov 21:13

A good person knows the rights of the poor, but; wicked people cannot understand such things.

Prov 29:7

If you want to be happy, be kind to the poor.

Prov 14:21

Meaning: Helping the poor is linked to living a life of justice. If you don't help the poor, then you'll pay for it one way or another. If you do, you'll be rewarded one way or another.

Other forms of charity

Jews believe that charity is any act of kindness. It's not just giving money. It might even be something as simple as visiting someone who has had a death in the family. Jews believe that it's important not to make the person you give charity to, feel embarrassed about it. They should be helped, but allowed to keep their dignity too.

Real Jews

A poem:

> Blessed is the Lord our God,
> King of the Universe.
> He shows me the hungry
> the poor
> the suffering.
>
> He gives me the job,
> the family
> the friends
> the freedom
>
> to choose
>
> to keep them all for me?
> Or share
> Like he shares his Universe with me.

Anon

Jewish charity in action

Tzedek is a Jewish charity. It started in 1990. It tries to do two things:

❶ 'To provide direct support to the developing world working towards the relief and elimination of poverty regardless of race or religion'.

❷ 'To educate people about the causes and effects of poverty and the Jewish obligation to respond' (their website).

The organisation says it is guided by Jewish ideas of right and wrong. The word tzedeka means charity. The word tzedek means justice. The two are linked. It believes that by helping others it is showing everyone God's love – which Jews are supposed to do. It also believes that charity helps to 'repair' the world (tikkun olam).

Jews don't think charity is just a matter of choice. It's an obligation – something you must do – if you want to show others what God is like.

Special times, special giving

Pesach and Shabbat Meals – Jews believe that you should, if you can, invite people who are poor and needy to share these meals with you.

Painting by Marc Chagall of a Jewish woman giving food to a poor man.

Bar/Bat Mitzvah – Many Jews have started donating money to charities as a way of marking these special events in a young person's life. Some Jews have said that you should spend a little less on the event itself, and give what you save to charity.

Sukkoth – This is a celebration of the harvest. Again, the poor should be invited to share in the meals in the sukkah. In the past, at harvest, farmers left a corner of the field for the poor. They could come and take what they wanted.

PAUSE & RECORD

- In your own words, explain why Jews, Muslims and Christians will all help charities which help people in religions which are different to theirs.

Giving back to God

Sikhs believe that everything good comes from God. Everything belongs to him. So it is your duty to share this with others. In this way, you give back to God what belongs to him anyway. Sikhs believe that you should give as much as you can. This is called 'vand chakna'. Sikhs believe they should give a tenth of their wealth to others. This is called 'Dasvandh'. This might be money, but it also could be your time and energy.

Give to God what belongs to God. One tenth of your time, your belongings, your income, your thoughts, one tenth of every act. Every act is blessed in which one tenth belongs to God and Guru.

Siri Singh Sahib

Sikhs also believe that you will receive God's blessing if you give Dasvandh. You might even find that what you have left after giving Dasvandh goes further than you thought!

At the end of every service in the Gurdwara, 'karah prashad' is given out. This is a mixture of butter, sugar, flour and water. It is given to everyone to show that all are one in God's eyes.

Also, in the Gurdwara, there is always a langar – a kitchen. At the end of every service a meal is prepared. This is shared between everyone who has attended the service. It is a free meal. In India, it could be the only meal the poor have. So, it is a way of caring for others and giving charity.

Sikhs believe that God cares for everyone, no matter who they are. But they also believe that it is up to every person to put God's love into practice by caring for others.

RewindRewind **Rewind**

In what ways is Sikh charity like the other faiths you've looked at in this unit?

Teaching from Sikh scriptures

He who refuses to have a poor person sit beside him commits an offence.

The Tanakhah-nama

Meaning: Sikhism began in India. The caste system meant that some people were treated very badly. If you were the lowest caste, higher castes might not even want to be near you, never mind help you. Guru Nanak didn't like this. He taught that everyone deserved kindness. So Sikhs help the poor when they can. They treat them as equals. It's wrong to treat them in any other way.

Other forms of charity

Sewa: Sikhs must help others in any way possible. This is a way of showing selflessness – instead of selfishness. It can even be something as simple as sweeping the floor of the Gurdwara. This is a way of showing that charity isn't just about giving money. It's about giving yourself in the sevice of others.

Real Sikhs

Panjit Singh works as a doctor in India. Every day he has a one-hour open clinic for the poor. He does not charge anything for this.

> *When I started this up, people said others would take advantage of me. People who could pay perfectly well would turn up, dressed in rags, for free treatment. This didn't happen. God blessed me with the skills to become a doctor. I pay him back by using these skills to help others.*

Sikh charity in action

Khalsa Aid was set up in Britain in 1999. It's based on the teachings of Bhai Kanaya Singh ji who would help those who had been injured in battle – no matter what they believed. Khalsa Aid sent help to Kosovo during the troubles in June 1999. It helps both Sikhs and non-Sikhs in Britain and abroad.

Special times, special giving

Baisakhi – This is the day when Sikhs are reminded that their role in life is as soldiers. They are soldiers who have to fight against injustice and unfairness.

- What do Dasvandh, Zakat and Christian tithing all have in common?

What do you know?

❶ What did Tom Monaghan do and why did he do it?

❷ Give two reasons why someone might give to charity.

❸ Give two reasons why someone might not give to charity.

❹ How could giving to charity make you feel 'less attached to wealth'?

❺ Why do some people think the National Lottery isn't good for charity?

❻ Name one charity you've looked at in this unit. How does it raise money and what does it do with it?

❼ Why might a Christian give to charity?

❽ What is Zakat?

❾ At what special events might Jews give to charity?

❿ What is Dasvandh?

What do you think?

❶ Design a poster for each of the faiths you've looked at in this section. This poster should explain to followers of that faith why they should give to charity, and how they should do so.

❷ Imagine you were put in charge of the National Lottery. What rules would you have about how you'd raise money, how prizes were allocated and where the money raised went. Write your list of guidelines.

❸ Imagine you were magically transported, right now, to a country where there is severe poverty. You are asked by the people who are suffering 'What have you done to help us?'. What would you say?

❹ Design a questionnaire which asks people which charities they support and why? Find out which are the most popular?

❺ On a display board write the heading:

'I think we should give to charity because...' Each person in your class should complete this sentence on a piece of paper and add it to the board.

❻ Draw up your own calendar for the year. Mark on this calendar special times and events for you (e.g. start of the football season!). Perhaps you could give a small sum to charity at these times.

action INTO

❶ Devise a presentation about the issues you've studied during this section. Maybe you could do this at your school assembly. You could structure it like this:

- Why charity is needed?
- Why should we help?
- What do the faiths say?
- What we should do?

Perhaps after this assembly you should organise a charity event for your school.

❷ Have a balloon debate in your class. Each person should represent one charity. Which is the most worthy of your support?

❸ Many popstars write songs to help raise money for charity. Write your own song for a chosen charity. Perhaps you could add some music and perform it too.

❹ Think about your own contributions to charity. Write an action plan for yourself! In this you should state clearly what you intend to do for charity over the coming year. It could be something quite simple – like having a sale of things you don't want any more. It could be more elaborate – like doing some volunteer work for a charity. Give yourself a target, either a sum of money, or an amount of time. After a year, write a review of how you've done. Who knows, it might even become a career!

Final Thoughts

This unit has looked at:

- Why we give to charity – or not.
- Why we should give to charity – or not.
- What religions have to say about giving to charity.

How have your views changed or developed as you've thought about the issues and people's responses? What can you do – what should you do?

Copy and complete the following:

Three things I could do to help charity are...

❶

❷

❸

Answer the following:

In this unit:

a. What have you enjoyed the best?

b. What did you not enjoy?

c. How good was your work?

d. What would you have liked to improve?

Now think of three more questions about charity that you'd like to find the answers to.

The name for a Jewish place of worship is a synagogue. The word 'synagogue' is not Hebrew – the language of the Jewish scriptures, but comes from the Greek word meaning 'bringing together'.

The Hebrew names used for a synagogue include: Bet ha Knesset (house of assembly) and Bet ha Midrash (house of learning).

Jews themselves usually call the synagogue a 'shul'. This is a Yiddish word. Yiddish is a special language spoken by some Jews which is a mixture of German and Hebrew but is written using Hebrew letters. The word 'shul' comes from the German word 'schule' which means 'school'. This word is used for synagogues as they are places where people go to learn about G-d.

In this section of the book the word God is written G-d. This is done out of respect for Jews. Jews believe that the name of their god is so holy that once they have written it down they can never destroy the piece of paper which it is written on. So, to avoid this problem, they write G-d – they know what these letters represent but they are not actually writing the name.

Different branches or groups of Jews have their own synagogues. In the United Kingdom there are Orthodox, Conservative, Reform and Liberal synagogues. Most of these are Ashkenazi synagogues. Ashkenazi Jews are those who originally came to Britain from northern and eastern Europe. However, there are also Sephardi synagogues for Jews whose origins are in Spain and Portugal.

Jews come together in the synagogue for worship, to learn more about G-d, to teach children and also to meet socially as a community.

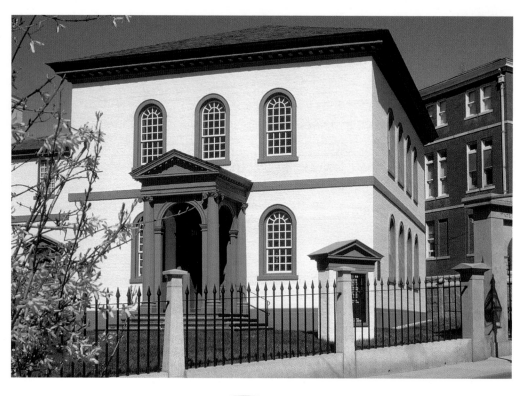

What do synagogues look like?

From the outside, synagogues are often very plain buildings. Sometimes the only way that we know that a building is a synagogue is because it has the symbol called the Star of David on a wall or in a window.

Synagogues are usually rectangular in shape, so that people can sit in a three-sided shape.

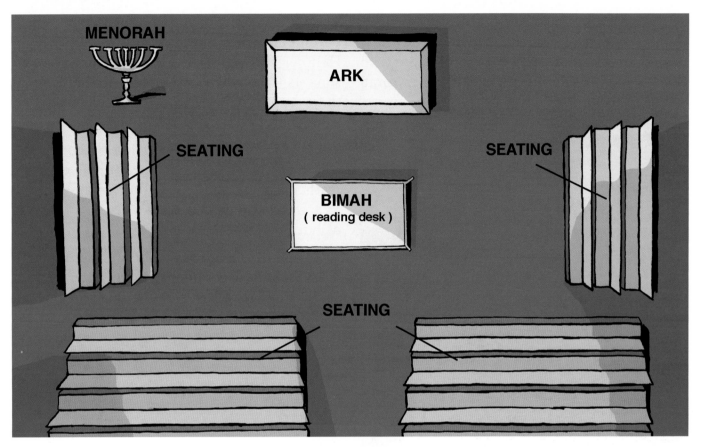

MENORAH

ARK

SEATING

SEATING

BIMAH
(reading desk)

SEATING

A plan of a synagogoue.

The seats all face the Aron Hakodesh or ark which is the most important part of any synagogue. The ark contains copies of the Jewish scriptures.

In the United Kingdom the ark is usually on the east wall of the synagogue. This means that when people face the ark they are also facing Jerusalem, the holy city of the Jews.

Rewind Rewind **Rewind**

Where do Ashkenazi and Sephardi Jews come from?

STOP & Think

➤ Why is a synagogue sometimes called a shul?

➤ Can you think of another religion where the place of worship has different names?

➤ Why do you think a synagogue is so important to the Jewish community?

➤ Explain why Jews write the word G-d rather than putting an 'o' in the middle of the word.

The most important feature of a synagogue is the ark. It is a cupboard with beautifully carved doors or a curtain embroidered with rich colours. Inside the ark are the Sefer Torah – the Torah scrolls.

The Sefer Torah scrolls, inside the ark.

The Sefer Torah are the first five books of the Jewish scriptures: Genesis, Exodus, Leviticus, Numbers and Deuteronomy. Jews believe that these books contain the actual words of G-d.

The scrolls are made of parchment, and on this parchment the five books are written in Hebrew. In Hebrew, the words only have consonants – the vowels are not written down and there is no punctuation. Hebrew is written from right to left across the page.

The scrolls are carefully copied by hand by a specially trained scribe using a turkey or goose feather. The parchment is attached at each end to a wooden pole called Etz Chaim – the Tree of Life.

The Sefer Torah are so important that they are dressed and decorated with a great deal of care. The type of covering used varies between Ashkenazi and Sephardic Jews, but both styles point to the fact that Jews have the greatest respect for the scrolls.

Ashkenazi scrolls are rolled up and tied with a linen band. Then they are wrapped in cover which is usually made of velvet. The two poles are longer than the cover. The bottom ends are used to carry the scrolls. The top of the poles are covered with rimmonim – a set of silver bells.

Over the mantle is a silver breastplate decorated with Jewish symbols such as pillars and crowns. A silver pointer in the shape of a long arm and hand with a pointing finger is hung on a chain over the top. This pointer, called a yad is used to follow the text of the scrolls without actually touching them.

Sephardic scrolls are placed in a wooden or metal case, which is carved or engraved. The case is in two halves and is hinged so that it can be opened like a book. The text can be read without the scroll having to be removed from the case.

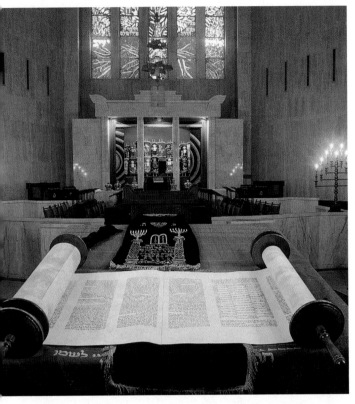

An open scroll on the bimah in the Great Synagogoue, Jerusalem.

In Orthodox synagogues men and women sit separately. The women sit in a gallery or behind a screen at the back of the synagogue. This is so that men and women do not distract each other while they are worshipping. In Progressive synagogues men and women usually sit together.

Most synagogues are relatively plain. The second of the Ten Commandments is:

> *'You shall not make for yourself an idol in the form of anything in heaven above or on the earth beneath or in the waters below. You shall not bow down to them or worship them; for I, the Lord your G-d, am a jealous G-d...'*
>
> *(Exodus 20:2–5)*

Above the Ark, is the ner tamid (eternal light) which symbolises the eternal presence of G-d. In front of the ark is the bimah. This is a reading desk from where the Torah Scrolls are read. The bimah faces the ark and also Jerusalem.

Because of this Jews do not have any pictures or statues in their synagogues. Some are decorated with quotations from the Torah or with simple designs such as patterns of leaves.

text message.........

Remember: Jews do not have any pictures or statues in their synagogues because this is forbidden by the Ten Commandments: 'You shall not make for yourself an idol in the form of anything in heaven above or on the earth beneath or in the waters below.'

✋ STOP & Think ❓

➤ How do other religions treat their holy books?

➤ Do you think it might be helpful for men and women to sit separately in a synagogue?

➤ Do you think that it is important to have very richly decorated places of worship?

Synagogues are very important buildings for Jews because they can meet together there and hear readings from the Torah and because they can pray together.

For Jews to pray together there must be at least ten men present. These ten are called a 'minyan'.

However, Jews can pray on their own at any time.

Before they enter the synagogue men and married women cover their heads and men put on a tallit (a prayer shawl) for morning prayer. The tallit is a long rectangle of cloth. On each of the four corners of the tallit are tzizit (tassels) each of which has five knots and eight threads.

In an Orthodox synagogue the services are almost entirely in Hebrew. The leader of a Jewish community is called a Rabbi which means 'teacher'. He will often read from the scrolls during a service and also give a sermon. The other parts of the service and are led by a chazan who has been trained to chant the words.

The Sefer Torah

The most important part of any service of worship is when the Sefer Torah is lifted from the Ark, carried to the **bimah** and read aloud.

On its way to the bimah – the scroll is carried in a procession around the synagogue. The congregation stand and follow the procession by turning so that they are always facing the scrolls. Men who are near to the scroll reach out to so that the tassels of their tallit touch the cover. They then kiss the tassels as a sign of devotion and respect.

When the Torah reaches the bimah the coverings are removed. It is unrolled a little, and

Jewish artifacts often found in synagogues. The seven-branched candlestick is called a menorah and is a symbol of Judaism. The light from the candles helps to remind worshippers of the presence of G-d. There are seven candles because the number '7' is a holy number for Jews and reminds them of the Bible story in which God creates the world in seven days.

then held up high and slowly turned around so that everyone can see the writing on the parchment.

The Torah is read during worship on Sabbaths and festivals and every Monday and Thursday. Readings take place at the end of morning worship and during the afternoon service. The whole of the Torah is read during the year. The last reading takes place on the festival of Simchat Torah (Rejoicing in the Torah) when the final words of the book of Deuteronomy are read in the same breath as the first words of the book of Genesis so that the cycle starts once more.

Shabbat service

The main service held in the synagogue is the Shabbat morning service on Saturday. (Shabbat is the name Jews usually use for the Sabbath.)

Shabbat begins, as all Jewish days, at sunset. Shabbat begins at sunset every Friday evening, and ends when seven stars appear in the sky on Saturday evening.

This service often last for two and a half to three hours. In a Progressive synagogue it will be slightly shorter.

Most synagogues have an organ but these are not played at Shabbat services because to do so would be a form of work and Jews are not allowed to work on Shabbat.

So at Sabbath services the singing is unaccompanied. The chazzan needs to be a good singer to lead the singing without any musical instruments being used.

text message.........

In the Ten Commandments it says: 'Remember the Sabbath day by keeping it holy. Six days you shall labour and do all your work, but the seventh day is a Sabbath to the Lord your G-d. On it you shall not do any work, neither you, nor your son or daughter, nor your manservant or maidservant, nor your animals, nor the alien within your gates. For in six days the Lord made the heavens and the earth, the sea, and all that is in them, but he rested on the seventh day. Therefore the Lord blessed the Sabbath day and made it holy.

(Exodus 20:8-11)

action INTO

❶ Draw a plan of a synagogue. Show the direction it is facing with a compass and then mark on it the main features which you would find there.

❷ Find out why Jews have to cover their heads when they go to a service in a synagogue.

❸ What other people cover their heads to worship and why?

Synagogues have several different names in Hebrew and each of these shows how the building can be used in many ways.

Bet Tefilah – the House of Prayer

Prayer is a very important part of Jewish life and worship. Jews pray to G-d at least three times a day. The design and layout of a synagogue is influenced by the need to pray facing Jerusalem.

One of the most important prayers in Judaism is called the Shema:

'Hear, O Israel: The Lord our G-d, the Lord is one. Love the Lord your G-d with all your heart and with all your soul and with all your strength. These commandments that I give you today are to be upon your hearts. Impress them on your children. Talk about them when you sit at home and when you walk along the road, when you lie down and when you get up. Tie them as symbols on your hands and bind them on your foreheads. Write them on the door-frames of your houses and on your gates.'

(Deuteronomy 6:4–9)

This prayer reminds Jews who they are and what G-d expects of them.

Bet ha Midrash – the House of Study

The synagogue is a place where people go to learn about their religion and to be taught about it. Synagogues have many different activities taking place. These may include: learning Hebrew, discussion groups, parent and children groups, and discussions about the weekly Torah readings. Most synagogues also run a school on Sundays where children learn Hebrew and learn more about their religion. A school like this is called a cheder. These schools prepare children for the Bar or Bat Mitzvah (Son or daughter of the Law). A boy usually becomes Bar Mitzvah when he is thirteen and he can then take part in services and be part of a minyan.

A boy studying for his Bar Mitzvah.

Bet ha Knesset – the House of Assembly

Synagogues are used by Jews as meeting places. Meetings do not always have to have a religious purpose and people may have parties and social events at the synagogue.

Bet Ha'am – the House of People

Finally, the synagogue is the place where services of worship are held.

The Mikveh

Another very important part of a synagogue is the mikveh. This is usually in a separate building. It is a deep pool of running water and is used for religious cleansing. Before a woman is married she goes to the mikveh. In one room she will shower and make sure that she is not wearing any make up or nail polish. Then she steps down into the mikveh and goes completely under the water three times. Each time she says:

'Blessed are you, O Lord our G-d, King of the universe who commands us to use the mikveh.'

After this she is spiritually clean and ready to be married. Married women use the mikveh regularly and many men also go there before the Jewish festivals. It is a very important part of Jewish life and of the synagogue.

action INTO

❶ Try to find out how Jews follow the instruction in the Shema to 'Tie them as symbols on your hands and bind them on your foreheads. Write them on the door-frames of your houses and on your gates.'

❷ Prepare a list of questions which you could use when asking a Jew why the synagogue is so central to Jewish life.
Use the answers from these questions to produce a table showing the response to each of the things you have asked.

❸ Find out what other religions may do which is similar to using a mikveh.

STOP & Think

➤ Why does a synagogue have so many different names?

➤ Where do Jewish children go to learn about their religion?

➤ What is a mikveh?

Some of the beliefs and practices of Judaism places Jews apart from other people.

Sometimes people say that because in the Bible, the Jews are called the 'chosen people' this means that Jews think they are better than non-Jews.

In fact, when G-d said that the Jews were the 'chosen people' it meant that they had a duty to work very hard in order to show other people what G-d wanted. They were not special in any way but had to try to give a good example to others.

One very important duty of all duties is to keep G-d's laws and in particular keeping the Sabbath.

Jews observe the Sabbath as a day of rest in honour of the day when G-d rested after he had finished the creation of the world.

> *'By the seventh day G-d had finished the work he had been doing; so on the seventh day he rested from all his work. And G-d blessed the seventh day and made it holy, because on it he rested from all the work of creating that he had done.'*
>
> *Genesis 2:2–3*

The Shabbat

The Sabbath or Shabbat begins at sunset on Friday evening, and ends when seven stars appear in the sky on Saturday evening.

On the Sabbath, Jews are forbidden to work or do any kind of business. There are 39 different laws which forbid work on the Sabbath - these include preparing food, washing, building, writing and lighting a fire.

These laws might seem as though they make life difficult, but Shabbat is seen as a day of rest. It is a happy occasion each week because families have the opportunity to spend time together and also have the time to worship G-d. So, Shabbat is a gift from G-d to the Jews.

Kashrut or Food Laws

Another way in which the community is brought closer together is the food laws which Jews have to follow.

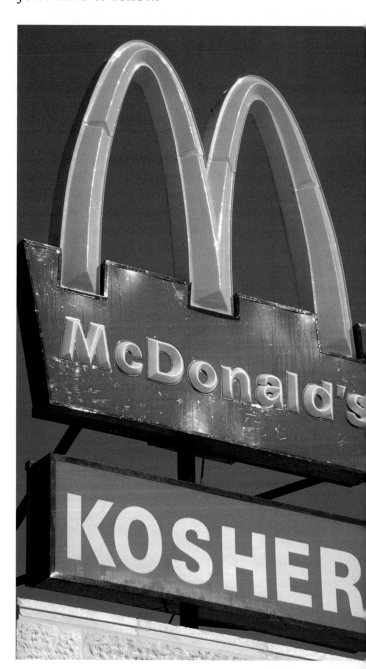

These laws are called kashrut – fit or suitable. So kosher food is food which is suitable for Jews to eat. Progressive Jews may not be as strict as Orthodox Jews but many still follow these rules.

The laws about Jewish food are found in the Torah. It is not clear why Jews have to follow these particular rules but they do so because that is what G-d taught them.

Jews are not allowed to eat pork or shellfish or any animal which eats dead meat. The meat which Jews do eat has to be killed by a special butcher who makes a single cut across the animal's throat whilst thanking G-d for the animal.

Also, Jews cannot eat meat and dairy products in the same meal:

> Do not eat anything you find already dead. You may give it to an alien living in any of your towns, and he may eat it, or you may sell it to a foreigner. But you are a people holy to the Lord your G-d. Do not cook a young goat in its mother's milk.

> **Deuteronomy 14:21**

A sense of community is very important for Jews. For hundreds of years Jews have been persecuted because of their faith. They had to leave the Holy Land of Israel in 70CE and since then most Jews have lived in other parts of the world. These Jewish communities are called the Diaspora (dispersion).

text message.........

Remember: The Holocaust, which Jews call Sho'ah, means destruction. Six million Jewish men, women, and children were killed by the Nazis during the Second World War. This was only one of the many persecutions which the Jews have faced during their history.

The worst disaster to come to the Jews was the Holocaust of the Second World War (1939–1945). During this time, six million Jews were put to death by the Nazis, the leaders of the Third Reich in Germany.

It is because of this suffering and the need to pray and live together that Jewish communities are so strong and the synagogue is so important to them.

Rewind Rewind **Rewind**

What does kashrut mean?

What types of food are Jews not allowed to eat?

What sort of things are Jews not allowed to do on the Sabbath?

For every religion, there are special places where people may go to worship. In Christianity this is often a church and Muslims go to a mosque. For Sikhs, wherever there is a copy of their holy scriptures, the Guru Granth Sahib Ji, the building becomes a gurdwara. Buddhists and Hindus may worship in a temple but they also have shrines at home where they can pray.

All religious believers can also pray at any time in any place. It is always more important to pray than to go to a special place of worship as all religions believe that their god will hear their prayers wherever they are.

Jews often pray spontaneously – whenever they feel that they should. Many of these prayers are called Berachot – blessings. A typical Berachot might be:

'Blessed are you, Lord our G-d, King of the universe who makes beautiful trees grow.'

These are short blessings which thank G-d for life and creation. Jews also say the Shema often as a reminder of the importance of G-d in every part of the lives.

When we learn about a synagogue and its special importance to the Jewish community we must also remember that many important aspects of Jewish worship take place at home.

The Jewish home

In a Jewish home, each door, except the bathroom, has a mezuzah on it. This is a small box which contains a scroll with the Shema written on it. Jews touch this as they pass to remember the prayer.

The laws of kashrut are put into operation in the home and young children will learn about their religion from their parents by the way in which they live their lives at home.

Many of the important Jewish festivals such as Shabbat, Pesach and Sukkot have special celebrations which also take place at home.

However, the synagogue is also very important in Jewish life as we have discovered. The synagogue contains the Sefer Torah and is the main place of community worship. It is usually where marriages and Bar Mitzvahs take place. Also the synagogue contains the mikveh which is an important part of Jewish spiritual life.

The synagogue also serves many other purposes in the community. There are synagogues in most cities in the United Kingdom and Jews will try to attend the synagogue whenever they can.

The Jewish Community

Today, many Jews do not live in Jewish communities and they may work with many non-Jews. By attending a synagogue Jews have the opportunity to meet each other and to share their beliefs and experiences. Jews are often concerned that if their children do not marry other Jews then the Jewish tradition will die.

Youth clubs and other organisations in the synagogues give young people the opportunity to meet each other.

A synagogue is special to a Jewish community not simply as a place to go to worship G-d, to hear the Torah being read and to pray but also because it provides somewhere where Jews can meet other Jews for worship and socially. It is the centre of the community.

A group of young Jewish people attend a summer camp organised by their synagogue. Being part of the community is very important to Jewish people.

STOP & Think

➤ Why is a Jewish home important?

➤ Why is the synagogue important for the Jewish community?

➤ Why might Jewish families want their children to meet other Jews?

INTO

❶ Try to find out how some Jewish festivals are celebrated in the home.

❷ From what you have learnt, write a short account explaining to a non-Jew why a synagogue is important to the community.

❸ Write about a particular place which is important to you and explain its importance.

What do you know?

❶ What words do Jews use for a synagogue?

❷ What is Yiddish?

❸ What does kashrut mean?

❹ What is a mikveh?

❺ What are the Sefer Torah?

❻ What was the Holocaust?

❼ What is the Shema?

❽ Why do men and women often sit separately in a synagogue?

❾ Why do Jews keep the Sabbath?

❿ What is a Berachot?

What do you think?

❶ Jews do not allow pictures of people in a synagogue. They say that pictures like this are forbidden. Why they do this?

❷ Why do you think attending a Sabbath morning service in a synagogue might be helpful to Jews?

❸ Think about the way in which the scrolls are treated. Why do you think Jews do this?

❹ What differences are there between a synagogue and other places of worship which you have learnt about?

End of Unit Activities

action INTO

❶ Find out how the Sabbath is celebrated in a Jewish home and write an account of this.

❷ Explain how keeping kosher might affect the way in which a Jew lives. You need to consider what happens when they are not at home.

❸ Try to find out more about the Holocaust and explain why it was such an important event for Jews.

❹ Write a short article in which a Jew explains why the synagogue is so important to them.

❺ Write a Berachot which thanks G-d for something special which you have seen or which has happened to you.

Final Thoughts

In this Unit you have learnt about the synagogue – the Jewish place of worship. think about and respond to the following.

• What have you learnt about the importance of the synagogue for the Jewish community?

• Explain how the way in which a synagogue is used might be a good example for other religions.

• How do you think that a place of worship might help the lives of followers of that religion?

The big picture

Tenjit is a Sikh. On most Sundays, she and the rest of her family go to the gurdwara, where they meet other members of the local Sikh community. They go to the gurdwara to worship God and to hear readings from the holy book of Sikhism, the **Guru Granth Sahib**.

- Why is the gurdwara a special place for Sikhs?

- What part does it play in religious and community life?

In this unit Tenjit talks about her gurdwara and what takes place there.

Sunday is not a specially holy day for Sikhs – they believe that God should be worshipped every day, not just on one day a week. But Sunday is the day when most people don't have to go to work or school, so it is the most convenient time in the week for people to get together.

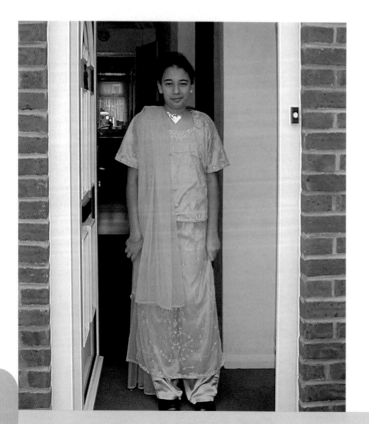

Language for learning

Gurdwara – is a place where Sikhs meet together to worship God. The name means 'the doorway of the guru'

Guru – is a special religious teacher

What do Sikhs wear to the gurdwara?

'Because I live in England, I usually wear English clothes. But when I go to gurdwara, I dress in a traditional Punjabi suit called shalwar kameez, and when I wear it, it reminds me of my culture. A lot of the women who go to my gurdwara wear Punjabi clothes all the time, at home and at work as well as to gurdwara, because it's what they're used to and they feel more comfortable.'

'I wear a wide scarf with my shalwar kameez, because when I'm inside the gurdwara, I'll need to cover my head. This is a new suit, my auntie brought it back from India for me.'

'My Dad and my brother wear turbans, as a sign that they are Sikhs. None of us cut our hair, because our religion teaches that if God has given you hair, why should you cut it? When my brother was smaller, he had his hair tied up in a knot on the top of his head, but now that he is older, he can manage to tie his own turban like the other men.'

Family life

'Family life is very important for Sikhs. We spend a lot of time with our relations. We always go to see them if they are ill, or on special occasions, or if they need any help, and they do the same for us. Some of my relations live nearby, and others live in India and in other countries too; we visit them as often as we can. Going to gurdwara is one of the things we like to do together, as a family.'

STOP & Think

➤ Do you think it is important for religious people to have one special day of the week? If so, does it matter which day is chosen?

text message.........

Outside the gurdwara, there is a flag with the Sikh symbol on it. The flag is called the Nishan Sahib. The flagpole is wrapped in saffron cloth, as a sign of respect, and every year, at a festival called Baisakhi, the flag and the cloth around the flagpole are replaced with new ones. Saffron is expensive to produce, and using this colour for the flag shows that Sikhs are ready to give up to God the things that they have.

God lasts for ever, because a circle has no beginning or end – people wear circular bangles, too, which remind them of the same thing. Sometimes people also say that the circle is a way of showing that God has made limits for us, so we have to try and live within God's rules and not do wrong things.

Outside the circle are two more swords, and these represent the belief that Sikhs should be prepared to defend what's right, even if it means putting themselves at risk sometimes. Sikhs often carry a little sword called a kirpan, to remind them of this; it's not a real sword that you could use as a weapon, because that would be against the law, the kirpan is just carried as a symbol and a reminder.

When the flag is flying on the gurdwara, it can be seen from quite a long way away. It lets people know that the gurdwara is there, in case they want to come. Everyone is welcome. It doesn't matter whether they are Sikh or not, or whether they are male or female, rich or poor. Sikhs believe that God made everyone equal, and doesn't have favourites.

Gurdwaras can be purpose built but often they are converted buildings, like Tenjit's:

The symbol on the flag is called the Khanda. In the middle of the Khanda symbol is a sharp sword, which reminds Sikhs of God's power and strength at the centre of their lives. There is a circle around it, which reminds them that

'When I was very little, we used to rent a building to use as a gurdwara, but it didn't belong to us. Other people used it for other things during the rest of the week. Then everyone got together to raise money, and now we own this building. We can keep our things here all the time.

It needs painting, so everyone in our community who can afford it is giving some money, and when we've got enough, we'll decorate it.'

The Khanda symbol

PLEASE TAKE YOUR SHOES OFF AND COVER YOUR HEAD BEFORE ENTERING THE HALLS.

TO CARRY AND CONSUME TOBACCO PRODUCTS DRUGS AND ALCOHOL IS STRICTLY PROHIBITED INSIDE GURDWARA PREMISES.

Signs outside Tenjit's gurdwara.

Entering the gurdwara

When people go into the gurdwara, they take off their shoes and cover their heads, to show respect for God. There are signs telling people not to bring alcohol or tobacco into the building, because it is against the Sikh religion.

STOP & Think

➤ Why do you think so many religions disapprove of smoking and drinking? Do you think they are right?

What happens inside the gurdwara?

Tenjit explains what happens at her gurdwara:

'After we've taken off our shoes and covered our heads, we go into the main prayer hall, which is called the **Darbar Sahib***. The first thing you notice is a raised platform with a canopy over it, and on this platform is our holy book, the Guru Granth Sahib. It's really important to us. When our religion first began, there were ten teachers, called* **gurus***, starting with Guru Nanak Dev Ji. Each of the gurus chose who was going to be the next guru. But the tenth guru, who was called Guru Gobind Singh Dev Ji, said that after his death, instead of having any more human teachers, there would be a book to teach us.'*

'We treat the Guru Granth Sahib with a lot of respect. Of course we don't worship the book – we worship God – but the teachings are very important for us. When we first go into the Darbar Sahib, we go up to the front and bow down in front of the Guru Granth Sahib. We leave an offering, usually some money but sometimes food or milk. We keep the book on silk cloths called **romallas***, and we cover it with cloths when it's not being used. During the service, someone stays with the Guru Granth Sahib, and waves a fan called a* **chauri***; it's just as if the book is a king on his throne and a servant is looking after him.'*

In the prayer hall there are pictures of the gurus around the walls. People can look at them during the service and think about what they did and what they taught.

text message.........

The Guru Granth Sahib is present at every Sikh service and special occasion. Every copy is the same. They all have 1430 pages, and the same hymns are found on the same page of every copy. It is written in Gurmurkhi, which means 'from the mouth of the Guru', and Sikhs believe that the Guru Granth Sahib contains the actual words spoken by the ten gurus. It is written in poetry. Some are meant to be said, and some are to be sung.

Not everything in the Guru Granth Sahib was written by Sikhs – some of its writings come from Hindus and Muslims. Some people think this is a bit strange. But Sikhs believe that there is truth in all religions, and that people all worship the same God and should respect each other's beliefs.

Language for learning

Darbar Sahib – the main prayer hall of the gurdwara

Guru Granth Sahib – the holy book of Sikhism

When people have made their offerings at the front, they sit down. Men and women sit separately. This isn't a religious rule, Sikhs believe that men and women are equal, but it's part of their culture. They think it's better if men and women sit apart in the gurdwara, because it makes it easier to concentrate on the words.

Everyone sits on the floor, and this shows that no one is any better than anyone else. People can't have good seats just because they're rich! When everyone is sitting down, they are below the Guru Granth Sahib, which shows respect and that they want to follow its teachings.

The service

'The service at gurdwara is quite long, but you don't have to be there all the time. You can just come for half an hour if that's all you can manage. It's quite informal, and no-one minds if there are people walking in and out. But you are supposed to be quiet, so that everyone can listen to the readings and prayers.'

The service is said and sung in Punjabi, which is the language most Sikhs speak. The person who leads the service and reads from the Guru Granth Sahib is called the **granthi**. Men or women can do this, it doesn't matter, as long as they have been taught how to do it properly.

Songs from the Guru Granth Sahib are sung by people called **ragis**, who sit lower than the book but a bit higher than everyone else so that everyone can hear them. They play Indian drums called **tabla**, and other instruments.

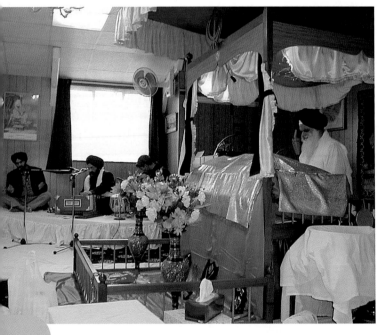

'When we hear the hymns and the readings, we learn about God and about how we should live. The Guru Granth Sahib teaches about all kinds of things. It has lots of different names for God, and we are encouraged to think about these names and to repeat them. We also hear stories which show us the right way to behave towards each other.'

When the service is coming to an end, people stand up to listen to the **ardas**, which is a prayer. They remember God and the gurus and people who have died because of their beliefs. They also say prayers for people in their community who are ill, and for the families of those who have died.

Then the granthi (the person doing the reading) opens the Guru Granth Sahib at random, and reads out the passage, which is God's special message for the day. After this, everyone receives some **karah prashad** as explained by Tenjit:

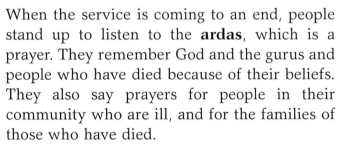

Language for learning

karah prashad – a special sweet food which is blessed and shared at the end of the service

Punjabi – the language most Sikhs speak

ragis – musicians

'You have to hold out both your hands, and someone comes and gives you a special sweet food which has been blessed. It's made with butter, flour, sugar and water. We all have some together, and it's a way of showing that we are all equal and we all receive blessings from God.'

A plan of a gurdwara.

1. Nishan Sahib (flag)
2. Entrance to gurdwara
3. Cloakroom
4. Washing areas
5. Prayer area for men
6. Prayer area for women
7. Pictures of gurus
8. Food and money donations
9. Area where ragis (musicians) sit
10. Guru Granth Sahib
11. Palki (canopy over Guru Granth Sahib)
12. Room for Guru Granth Sahib
13. Langar room /kitchen

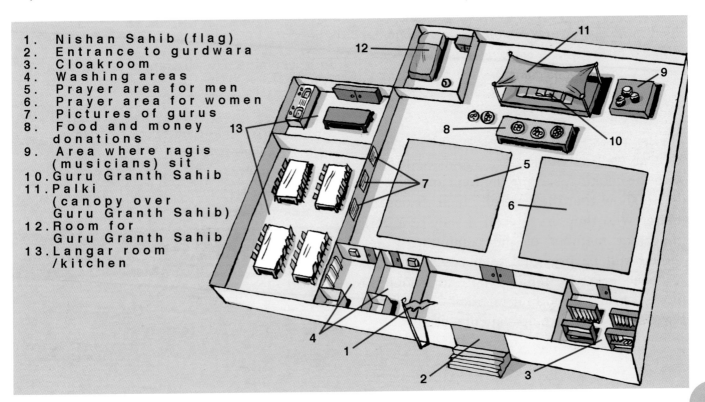

'When the service is over, we all go into the next room where the langar is served. The langar is a meal for everyone. Each week, families take it in turns to get it ready. Usually, you have a turn to make the langar when it's a special occasion for your family, like a birthday or a wedding anniversary, and your relations come the day before and help you to get all the food ready. We like it when it's our turn to prepare the langar.'

The langar is prepared and served by anyone. Men as well as women are supposed to help with the cooking, serving the food and clearing up, to show that they are all equal. It doesn't matter who they are – even if they're a very important member of the community, they should still be prepared to make a meal for someone else. As Tenjit says, 'you shouldn't think,"I'm too important for that", you should always be ready to help someone else.'

The food is always vegetarian. Quite a lot of Sikhs are vegetarian, but they don't have to be, it's not a religious rule. Vegetarian food is served at the langar so that it doesn't offend anyone, everyone can join in, whatever their beliefs are.

Tenjit explains why the langar is important for Sikhs:

'It's a way of sharing what God has given us with everyone. In India, poor people come to the gurdwara because they know they can get something to eat. Looking after other people is a very important part of our beliefs – we call it **sewa**.*'*

• Why is sharing the langar together important for Sikhs?

'When we eat our food, we still sit separately, with men and women at different tables. When we've finished eating, it's time to go home. If you haven't prepared the langar, you're supposed to do something to help, like wiping the tables or washing up.'

Although Sikhs worship at the gurdwara mainly on Sundays, this doesn't mean that it stays empty for the rest of the week. It is used for Punjabi classes, because a lot of children who were born in England don't know how to read and write Punjabi. It is also used for the community; for example, members of the gurdwara use the building to look after elderly people in the community.

Back at home

Some Sikhs have copies of the Guru Granth Sahib **(a)** at home, as well as at the gurdwara. They keep a special place for it, usually a spare bedroom. Then they can read it every day when they do their prayers.

Below are some of the things found in Tenjit's home.

'We also keep objects around the house to remind us of our beliefs. The ik onkar symbol **(b)** tells us that there is only one God. You often see this in Sikh homes and cars. And the pictures of the gurus **(c)** remind us of all the things they taught.'

(b)

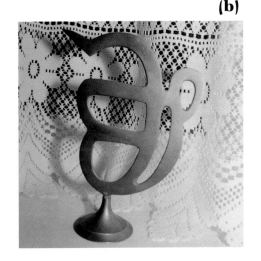

(a)

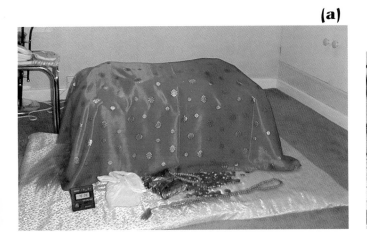

(c)

WHAT MAKES A GURDWARA SPECIAL FOR SIKHS?

End of Unit Activities

What do you know?

❶ What does the word 'gurdwara' mean?

❷ What is the Khanda symbol, and what does it represent?

❸ Why are Sikhs not meant to cut their hair?

❹ What do Sikhs do as a sign of respect, before they go into the gurdwara?

❺ What is the name for the main prayer hall of the gurdwara?

❻ What is the Guru Granth Sahib Ji?

❼ How is respect shown for the Guru Granth Sahib Ji during the gurdwara service?

❽ How do Sikhs behave at gurdwara to show their beliefs that everyone is equal?

❾ **a.** What is karah prashad?

b. What is the langar?

c. Why is the food served at gurdwara vegetarian?

❿ What is the gurdwara used for when there isn't a service going on?

What do you think?

❶ What do you think are the advantages and disadvantages of having a human religious teacher?

❷ What are the advantages and disadvantages of having a book as a teacher?

❸ Do you think people are really equal, whether they are men or women, rich or poor? Give reasons for your answer.

action INTO

❶ Write a leaflet as a guide for visitors to the gurdwara. Explain what you should wear and how you should behave when you enter the building, Explain what goes on during the service and afterwards.

❷ Visit the website www.sikhs.org, and find out about the Golden Temple in Amritsar, which is the most famous Sikh gurdwara in the world. Look at the 'virtual tour'. Make a poster about the Golden Temple for display, using maps, description and artwork.

❸ Draw the plan of the gurdwara from p73, and write a detailed key for it, explaining the different features.

The Golden Temple in Amritsar, India.

Index